# MATHEMATICS CONTENT FOR ELEMENTARY AND MIDDLE SCHOOL TEACHERS

**BARBARA RIDENER**

*Florida Atlantic University*

**PENELOPE FRITZER**

*Florida Atlantic University*

PEARSON

Boston   New York   San Francisco   Mexico City
Montreal   Toronto   London   Madrid   Munich   Paris
Hong Kong   Singapore   Tokyo   Cape Town   Sydney

**Series Editor:** *Traci Mueller*
**Marketing Manager:** *Elizabeth Fogarty*
**Editorial Assistant:** *Krista E. Price*
**Production Administrator:** *Marissa Falco*
**Electronic Composition:** *Omegatype Typography, Inc.*
**Composition and Prepress Buyer:** *Linda Cox*
**Manufacturing Buyer:** *Andrew Turso*
**Cover Administrator:** *Jill Winitzer*

For related titles and support materials, visit our online catalog at www.ablongman.com

Between the time Website information is gathered and then published, it is not unusual for some sites to have closed. Also, the transcription of URLs can result in typographical errors. The publisher would appreciate notification where these errors occur so that they may be corrected in subsequent editions.

Ridener, Barbara.
    Mathematics content for elementary and middle school teachers / Barbara Ridener, Penelope Fritzer.
        p. cm.
    Includes bibliographical references and index.
    ISBN 0-205-40799-4 (pbk.)
        1. Mathematics—Study and teaching (Elementary)—Standards—United States. 2. Mathematics—Study and teaching (Middle School)—Standards—United States.   I. Fritzer, Penelope Joan.   II. Title.

QA13.5.R53 2004
372.7'02'1873—dc21                                              2003051826

Printed in the United States of America

10  9  8  7  6  5  4  3  2  1        07  06  05  04  03

*This book is dedicated to*
*Eric Ridener and to our children, Eric, Stephanie, and Shelby*
*and to*
*Joseph Gannon Bland and Elizabeth Fritzer*
*Many thanks to Dr. Judith Covington, Dr. Jill Mizell, and Dr. Letitia*
*Bridges, for their myriad prompt and helpful suggestions*

# CONTENTS

# PREFACE: A WORD TO THE READER

This book is a short primer in content to be used by the hard-pressed elementary or middle school math teacher as a quick reference to math knowledge and concepts. Though it may not be all-inclusive or relevant for every grade level, this book is relevant for any teacher wishing to be better informed and more confident about teaching mathematics. Many states are strengthening their math content in the younger grades as part of the standards movement, and this book will help teachers gain the confidence to keep up with and integrate newly required content.

For reasons of space, this book does not detail each state's requirements individually. Based broadly on the national standards, it gives the teacher enough general mathematical information to cover most states' standards. It also gives a broad enough overview of mathematical knowledge to allow the teacher to find information on important concepts, to see where significant moments in mathematical history fit chronologically, and to help in the teacher's own understanding of mathematical ideas and concepts.

This is not a methods book. There are many good mathematics methods books on the market that address, for example, interesting ways of students learning about division or elementary geometry. Rather, this book is aimed at raising the content knowledge of the teacher—often a problem with elementary education majors because the many pedagogy courses they must take frequently crowd out content courses. Additionally, even when specific math courses are required of elementary majors, they frequently memorize enough formulae to get them through exams, but often retain little in the way of mathematical understanding. As a result, despite its major place in standardized testing and the subsequent amount of class time spent on it, mathematics is often poorly and grudgingly taught at the elementary level, and experience indicates that lack of teacher knowledge and confidence is a major factor in the weakness of elementary mathematics teaching. This book is intended to address that lack of knowledge. Problems with innumeracy (mathematical illiteracy) plague the American public, including many teachers who are more comfortable teaching elements of reading and the liberal arts. Thus, a short primer in math content is important to build teacher confidence—which should translate into teacher, and, subsequently, student enthusiasm.

The book is organized into eleven chapters: A Short History of Mathematics; Number Sense and Concepts; Whole Number Operations; Fractions, Decimals, and Percents; Algebraic Thinking; Measurement; Geometry and Spatial Sense; Data Analysis and Probability; Problem Solving and Logical Reasoning; Mathematics, Technology, and Teaching; and Communication, Connections, and Representation. All of the chapters address what the elementary teacher (including sixth grade, often designated middle school) needs to know. The biggest emphasis is on understanding number sense, concepts, and operations— which will be most relevant to many teachers. There is also a substantial index, as well as lists of content resources.

We would like to thank the following reviewers for their suggestions: Judith Covington, Louisiana State University at Shreveport; Jill A. Mizell, State University of West Georgia; and Letitia Bridges, State University of West Georgia.

# CHAPTER 1

# WHY STUDY MATHEMATICS?

Many people find mathematics abstract and intimidating but are interested in their or their families' personal need to measure something or keep track of their finances. Measurement and finance are often the most pragmatic aspects of mathematics with which many people have contact. Much mathematics is an expansion of that knowledge, extended to other concepts—both concrete and abstract.

Communications, travel, space exploration, labor-saving devices, entertainment, and a myriad of other endeavors are different for modern humans than in the past, due to the mathematical and scientific advances of the last few hundred years, and particularly of the twentieth century. As humankind is poised at the beginning of the twenty-first century, math is increasingly important and influential. However, people may not be conscious of the importance of mathematics in their understanding of, and decisions about, their lives and their material goods. They are at an enormous disadvantage if they do not at least have a basic understanding of mathematical concepts, and some recognition of how mathematics affects aspects of their lives.

While the mathematics of everyday life (such as balancing one's checkbook, paying for groceries, and calculating mileage), are essential, a more in-depth knowledge is more abstract and far less relevant to everyday life, but absolutely necessary for future scientists and engineers. Computers, space exploration, and many scientific inventions and discoveries, including perspective in art, would not be possible without high-level, abstract mathematics. The rigorous formulae and mental discipline required in mathematics are also thought to create foundations for clear, logical thinking in almost any other subject.

Even our own American freedoms—born out of eighteenth-century rationalism and political philosophy, which in turn grew out of John Locke's seventeenth-century idea of "natural right"—are based on the concept of mathematical "laws" and on the laws of the universe.

Ideas and knowledge about our world, often based on mathematical concepts, help make us truly and uniquely human. The importance of knowledge, and control and dissemination of that knowledge, has driven the development of more intensive mathematical curricula in recent years and has resulted in vast differences and opportunities between those who move easily in the world of knowledge and those who struggle with it. Ideally, knowledge is far-reaching, democratic, and accessible to all. Hence, the importance of teachers knowledgeable about math content in every school, not just in affluent schools, which often offer higher pay and better working conditions.

## READINGS FOR STUDENTS

Burns, M. (1998). *Math: Facing an American Phobia.* Sausalito, CA: Marilyn Burns Education Associates.

Martinez, J. and Martinez, N. (1996). *Math without Fear.* Boston, MA: Allyn & Bacon.

Tobias, S. (1978). *Overcoming Math Anxiety.* Boston: Houghton Mifflin.

# CHAPTER 2

# A SHORT HISTORY OF MATHEMATICS

Although humankind's need for counting probably initiated the development of mathematics, many early societies did not count in the same fashion as people do today. Rather, most early societies had indications only for the idea of "one" and the idea of "many." Eventually, the decimal system developed—probably based on the idea of counting on ten fingers. The ancient Egyptians, faced with the problem of marking out the area where the Nile flooded every year, developed early geometry. Egyptian numerals were based on the decimal system and the Egyptians had a fairly sophisticated understanding of the properties of triangles and circles, contrasting with their awkwardness in expressing simple fractions.

Both the Egyptians and the ancient Babylonians could do various number calculations, including multiplication and weight measurement, and the more sophisticated Babylonians even had primitive forms of algebra and fractions by about 1700 B.C. Sumerians and Babylonians used multiplication and division, developed the idea of place value, and created tables to compute interest.

The Greeks are famous for their own developments in mathematics. By the fifth and sixth centuries B.C., Greek mathematics were quite sophisticated. For example, Thales's four propositions are the basis for some modern geometry: a circle is bisected by its diameter; the angles at the base of an isosceles triangle are equal in measure; two intersecting pairs of straight lines form two pairs of equal angles; and an angle inscribed in a semi-circle is a right angle. Pythagoras is thought to have proven the theorem named after him, although it was known to the ancient Babylonians as well. Euclid laid the basis of modern geometry with his *Elements of Geometry,* based on axioms (basic truths used as starting points) and theorems (which must be proved). However, the greatest of the Greek mathematicians was

Archimedes, who in the fifth century B.C. worked out the value of *pi* (making it possible to measure a circle), invented a basic form of calculus, and discovered the value of the lever.

Alexander the Great's conquest of most of the known world (much of southern Europe, North Africa, and the Middle East) in the fourth century B.C. spread Babylonian and Greek methods throughout that world, culminating in Ptolemy's calculations on the solar system in the third century A.D. When the Roman Empire later ruled the same area, starting in 27 B.C., Roman numerals were widely used, but they were hard to work with because they are not tied to place value.

Hindu astronomy after the fifth century A.D. included the concept of trigonometry and place value notation. After the 600s, the Islamic world continued advancements in mathematics, using both eastern and western components, including the establishment of so-called "Arabic numbers" (actually Arabic-Hindu), the number system that spread in the tenth and eleventh centuries A.D. and is now used around the modern world.

By the 1500s, the great discoveries in mathematics were linked with major discoveries in physics and astronomy in Europe. In the sixteenth and seventeenth centuries, Copernicus, Kepler, and Galileo helped organize human knowledge of the solar system and began to map it based on mathematical ideas that indicated, for example, the paths of planets and comets.

In the early part of the seventeenth century, the Frenchmen Rene Descartes and Pierre Fermat developed analytical geometry, which combined the ideas of algebra and geometry. Analytical geometry uses coordinates (the meeting place of two or three lines labelled *x, y,* and *z,* depending on whether the point being located is two-dimensional or three-dimensional) to locate points in space. Later in the seventeenth century, Isaac Newton and Gottfied Leibnitz, working independently, each invented a version of calculus. This led to later advances, including Newton's law of gravity, derived from applying math to the physical world.

The focus shifted as mathematical discoveries advanced over the years. In the twentieth century, Bertrand Russell and Alfred North Whitehead emphasized symbolic logic and abstract axiomatic concepts, while at the same time, the practical use of mathematics was more widespread than ever. Albert Einstein used mathematics to create his famous theory of relativity and to make calculations that helped advance space science. Francis Bacon, the Renaissance scientist, wrote that "Good science is useful science," and, reinforcing that statement, mathematic calculations have improved the accuracy of ballistics, navigation (leading to space exploration), communications (particularly in computers), and many other aspects of science and daily life.

## READINGS FOR STUDENTS

Bruno, L. C. and Baker, L. W. (1999). *Math and Mathematics: The History of Math Discoveries around the World. Volumes A–H and I–Z.* Seattle, WA: Gall Group.

Franco, B. (1999). *Fourscore and 7: Investigating Math in American History.* Pacific Palisades, CA: Goodyear Publishing Co.

Glasthal, J. B. (1999). *American History Math.* New York: Scholastic.

Landon L. (1999). *American History Mysteries.* New York: Scholastic.

## WEBSITES

**Math History for Kids**
http://www-groups.dcs.st-and.ac.uk/~history/

**Mathematicians' Biographies**
http://www-groups.dcs.st-and.ac.uk/~history/BiogIndex.html

# CHAPTER 3

# NUMBER SENSE AND CONCEPTS

## COUNTING

It is, perhaps, difficult as an adult to really think about the act of counting. Rarely does a person remember what it was like not to know how to count. Therefore, it may be hard to remember the intricacies involved.

Counting is learned first through the memorization of the sequence of counting numbers, a process called "rote counting." Through extended practice and repetition, the number name sequence is memorized. Rote counting is the process of reciting the sequence of counting numbers, "one, two, three,...," and is the initial step in learning to count. The sequence is memorized, but there is no initial connection to concrete objects. Instead, rote counting is an act that involves only communication and memory.

Once number names can be connected with objects, "rational counting" has begun. Rational counting is the process of correctly attaching the sequence to discrete (particular) objects. During rational counting the appropriate one-to-one correspondence is achieved, as each item is assigned one, and only one, number name. The number names are connected with the objects being counted, while the person is saying "one, two, three, four,...." If a particular object is the third counted, that object may not also be the second—each object is assigned a specific number name, so the counting continues from one number to another without repetition of any individual number.

Another aspect of rational counting is that the number name sequence is used in the correct order—the order learned during the rote counting stage. The order must be stated correctly for the counter to be said to have achieved the ability to count rationally.

The final part of the rational counting process is knowing that the last number stated is the number of objects in the set. This understanding is essential in beginning to learn to add and subtract numbers.

## NUMBER SETS

### Counting Numbers

When a person learns to count, the numbers used are "counting numbers," also known as "natural numbers." These are the set of numbers {1, 2, 3,…} that correlate to objects that are counted. They are the first numbers a person uses to count because the values represent discrete quantities.

### Whole Numbers

The next set of numbers a person learns is whole numbers. Whole numbers are the natural numbers plus zero. The set of whole numbers is written as {0, 1, 2, 3,…}. Whole numbers are the set that students learn prior to operations such as addition and subtraction.

Zero is a number that is not immediately understandable for children, at least partly because it is not a value that can be modeled with objects. The value of zero is learned by connecting it to states of existence; for example, if there are zero beans in a cup, there are no beans in the cup. It is the number that represents the absence of objects. The concept of zero is quite sophisticated, and it is a concept that many ancient cultures did not have.

### Integers

Integers are the set of numbers that consist of whole numbers and their opposites. They are the set {…, –3, –2, –1, 0, 1, 2, 3,…}. This set usually is not taught until the student is in the intermediate grades.

### Rational Numbers

Rational numbers are the set of numbers that include fractions and decimals. Formally, the definition often states that they are the set of numbers that can be written as "a over b" where $a$ and $b$ are integers, and $b$ is not equal to zero. In terms of a number line, the rational numbers exist in the spaces between the integers, as well as including the integers themselves.

### Irrational Numbers and Real Numbers

Real numbers are the set of all of the numbers (except imaginary numbers, which ordinarily would not be taught until high school).

Irrational numbers are non-repeating and non-terminating decimals that cannot be written as "a over b." For example, the square root of two is an irrational number.

All of the number sets can be illustrated in a diagram that represents their relationships to one another:

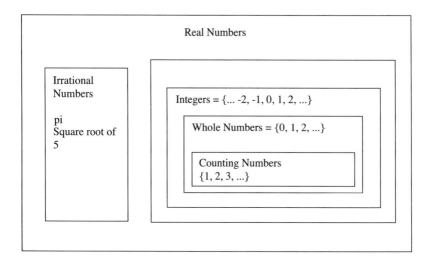

## TYPES OF COUNTING, NUMERALS, AND MODELS

There are various stages of counting that one passes through when developing proficiency. These include counting on, counting back, and skip counting. In addition, there are at least two common numeral systems used—Roman and Arabic—and there are various models used to represent value.

### Counting All

"Counting all" is the process used prior to conserving numbers when a person is unable to recall or use the quantity of a given set in order to combine it with another set. For example, given a set of five objects, if the quantity is not immediately recognized, they are counted, "One, two, three, four, five." However, if two more objects are added to the set, to find the total, the entire set is recounted starting with one, "One, two, three, four, five, six, seven."

## Counting On

From counting all, the person progresses to the process of "counting on." Counting on is the ability to continue counting from a given number. For example, given the number 12, the counting begins with 13 and continues 14, 15, and so on. Counting on is not always learned intuitively or through direct instruction; however, once a person "conserves numbers," he or she is able to count on easily.

The "conservation of numbers" is the association of the final number stated when counting a group of objects with the number of the objects in the group. This association means that although the objects may be rearranged, the number associated with the group remains the same. It also means that if a few more objects are added to the group, counting begins with the associated number, and all objects do not have to be recounted. Understanding this concept simplifies basic addition and subtraction.

## Counting Back

"Counting back" is simply counting in reverse order. It is recalling or memorizing the number sequence in a different order, so it is learned by rote. As comfort with the number system develops, counting back exemplifies the person's knowledge of that system. Counting back is a necessary precursor to subtraction.

## Skip Counting

"Skip counting" is the process of counting by groups of numbers. As with counting back, facility with skip counting is initially a result of memorizing a sequence. Twos, fives, tens, and hundreds are the initial and most common groups used for skip counting. In addition, skip counting is a precursor to recognizing even numbers and being able to count money.

## Numbers and Numerals

It is important to recognize the difference between number and numeral. "Number" refers to a concept, a quantity that may be counted and operated on. A "numeral" is the symbol that is used to represent a number, as with Roman or Arabic-Hindu numerals, for example.

## Place Value

Our number system is a place value system. This means that the position of a number represents its value. In the following numbers—2, 23, and 234—each of the 2s has a different value because it is in a different position each time. So the value of the position or the place, together with the value of the numeral, is integral in determining the value of the number.

There are specific rules for grouping and trading in the number system. Each group has a base of ten. This means that once we have ten of something, we group them together to make a new group. This grouping also represents each of the positions in our place value system. In 234, the 2 is in the hundreds place, which is ten times more than the tens place. The 3 is in the tens place in this example, and the tens are ten times more than the ones place, which is where the 4 is in this example.

The number 300 equals 30 tens, which equals 300 ones. The relationship that is created by our base of ten allows us to establish patterns and connections within our number system that facilitate written computation.

The other thing that is provided by the base of ten is that there are ten numerals that make up our system. Zero through nine are arranged in different places and different combinations to represent any possible discrete quantity.

As noted previously, zero represents the lack of a quantity, so it is sometimes called a "placeholder." Our number system is one of the few number systems to use a symbol to represent zero.

## Roman Numerals

The Roman numeral system is not a place value system, but a positional system. It is also an "additive system," since "I" represents one and, adding another marker, "II" represents two. The values of the numerals are combined together for the total value of a number. This system also is subtractive: if a smaller value comes before a larger value, the smaller value is subtracted from the larger for the total value. For example, IV equals four, but VI equals six. Furthermore, the Roman numeral system does not have a symbol that represents zero; and the symbol for ten is X, which has no relationship to the symbol for one.

**Value of Roman Numerals**

| ROMAN NUMERAL | VALUE OF NUMERAL |
|:---:|:---:|
| I | 1 |
| V | 5 |
| X | 10 |
| L | 50 |
| C | 100 |
| D | 500 |
| M | 1000 |

# PROPORTIONAL AND NON-PROPORTIONAL MODELS

## Proportional Models

With a proportional model, the size of the model is in proportion to the quantity being represented. For example, a 10 is 10 times larger than a 1, and a 100 is 10 times larger than 10 and 100 times larger than 1. Many different models are used to represent a variety of quantities. Discrete models or objects are individual items that are not connected and can be counted. Discrete models are one type of proportional model, in which the size of the object is proportional to the number being modeled. Proportional models are the easiest types of models to use when thinking about values.

## Non-Proportional Models

Understanding non-proportional models is essential to further understanding the complexities of our numeration system. In non-proportional models, the relationship of the object is determined by an attribute other than size. Colored chips that each have a different value are an example of a non-proportional model, since the color of the chip, rather than its size, determines its value. Money is another non-proportional model. Our monetary system is written as a decimal system, which is a base-ten place value system. However, the size and value of our coins and dollar bills are not proportional to their values.

## READINGS FOR STUDENTS

Adler, D. A. and Ross, L. (1975). *Base Five*. New York: Thomas Y. Crowell Publishers.
Adler, D. A. and Barton, B. (1977). *Roman Numerals*. New York: Thomas Y. Crowell Publishers.
Aker, S. and Karlin, B. (1990). *What Comes in 2's, 3's, and 4's?* New York: Simon & Schuster.
Anno, M. and Anno, M. (1977). *Anno's Counting Book*. New York: Thomas Y. Crowell Publishers.
Anno, M. and Anno, M. (1982). *Anno's Counting House*. New York: Philomel Books.
Aylesworth, J. and Young, R. (1988). *One Crow: A Counting Rhyme*. New York: J. B. Lippincott Co.
Bang, M. (1983). *Ten, Nine, Eight*. New York: Greenwillow Books.
Barnes-Murphy, R. (1988). *One, Two, Buckle My Shoe: A Book of Counting Rhymes*. New York: Little Simon.
Brenner, B. and O' Keefe, M. T. (1984). *Snow Parade*. New York: Crown Publishers.
Bright, R. (1985). *My Red Umbrella*. New York: William Morrow.
Bruna D. (1984). *I Can Count*. Los Angeles: Price/Stern/Sloan Publishers.
Calmenson, S. and Appleby, E. (1982). *One Little Monkey*. New York: Parents Magazine Press.
Calmenson, S. and Chambliss, M. (1984). *Ten Furry Monsters*. New York: Parents Magazine Press.
Campana, M. (1983). *The Saggy Baggy Elephant's Great Big Counting Book*. New York: Golden Press.
Carle, E. (1990). *1, 2, 3 to the Zoo*. New York: Philomel Books.
Chandler, J. (1980). *The Poky Little Puppy's Counting Book*. Racine, WI: Western Publishing Co.
Christelow, E. (1989). *Five Little Monkeys Jumping on the Bed*. New York: Clarion Books.
Corbett, G. (1982). *What Number Now?* New York: Dial Books for Young Readers.
Crews, D. (1986). *Ten Black Dots*. New York: Greenwillow Books.
Cristaldi, K. (1996). *Even Steven and Odd Todd*. New York: Cartwheel Books.
Dunrea, O. (1989). *Deep Down Underground*. New York: Macmillan Publishing Co.
Franco, B. (1999). *"Counting Caterpillars" and Other Math Poems*. New York: Scholastic.
Giganti, Jr., P. (1992). *Each Orange Had 8 Slices: A Counting Book*. New York: Greenwillow Books.
Gillen, P. B. (1987). *My Signing Book of Numbers*. Washington, D.C.: Kendell Green Publications.
Goldborough, J. (1983). *Numbers*. Teaneck, NJ: Sharon Publications.
Greenes, C. (1999). *Hot Math Topics Number Sense*. Palo Alto, CA: Dale Seymour Publishing.
Howard, K. and Smollin, M. J. (1979). *I Can Count to One Hundred...Can You?* New York: Random House.
Hughes, S. (1985). *When We Went to the Park*. New York: Lothrop, Lee & Shepard Books.
Johnston, T. and Young, E. (1987). *Whale Song*. New York: G. P. Putnam's Sons.

Law, F., Chandler S. and Farman, J. (1985). *Mouse Count.* Milwaukee, WI: Gareth Stevens.

Oechli, K. (1980). *Too Many Monkeys: A Counting Rhyme.* New York: Golden Press.

Reiss, J. J. (1971). *Numbers.* New York: Bradbury Press.

Samton, S. W. (1985). *The World from My Window: A Counting Poem.* New York: Crown Publishers.

Schwartz, D. H. and Kellogg, S. (1993). *How Much is a Million?* New York: Mulberry Books.

Turner, P. (1999). *Among the Odds and Evens.* New York: Farrar Straus Giroux.

Wadsworth, O. A. and Rae, M. M. (1986). *Over in the Meadow: A Counting-out Rhyme.* New York: Viking Kestrel.

Wahl, J. and Wahl, S. (1985). *I Can Count the Petals of a Flower.* Reston, VA: National Council of Teachers of Mathematics.

Winik, J. T. (1986). *Fun with Numbers.* Milwaukee, WI: Penworthy.

## WEBSITES

**NM Multiplication: An Adventure in Number Sense**
www.naturalmath.com/mult/

**Simply Number Sense!**
library.thinkquest.org/17888/opening.shtml

**The Math Forum—Math Library—Number Sense/About Numbers**
mathforum.org/library/topics/number_sense/

**Number Sense**
www.ceemast.csupomona.edu/mathstandards/ strands/numbersense.html

**Math Number Sense Math Lesson Plan, Thematic Unit, Activity,...**
www.lessonplanspage.com/MathNumberSense1.htm

**Number Sense and Numeration**
www.linktolearning.com/number_sense.htm

**Number Sense Software Programs, Worksheets, Place Values,...**
www.dositey.com/math/numfactk2.htm

**Simply Number Sense!**
library.thinkquest.org/17888/off_hm.shtml

**Number Sense**
linux1.ncktc.tec.ks.us/~usd298/Math/

**Grades Pre-K–2: Number and Operations**
standards.nctm.org/document/chapter4/numb.htm

**Lesson Tutor: Mathematics: Grade 5: Number Sense and Numeration...**
www.lessontutor.com/ltnumber5home.html

**A Lesson Plans Page Math Lesson Plan, Thematic Unit, Activity,...**
www.lessonplanspage.com/MathNumberSenseNumerationK3.htm

**Number Sense Every Day**
www.learnnc.org/newlnc/beacon.nsf/doc/numsense0402-1

**Lesson Tutor: Introducing Number Sense and Numeration**
www.lessontutor.com/NSN1.html

**Math**
www.edselect.com/math.htm

**Creative Mathematics Seminars, Mathematics in the Elementary...**
www.creativemathematics.com/seminars/elementary.htm

**Lesson Plans—Multiplication Presentation**
www.sun.com/aboutsun/comm_invest/ogp/lessons/colorado/mtv/
multiplicationPresentation.html

**Creative Mathematics Seminars, Teaching Mathematics Through...**
www.creativemathematics.com/seminars/mathlit.htm

**NCTM Illuminations**
illuminations.nctm.org/lessonplans/3-5/count/

**Math**
www.neillsville.k12.wi.us/abel/Math.htm

**Roman Numerals 101 Oliver S. Lawrence**
www.cod.edu/people/faculty/lawrence/romaindx.htm

**Math Forum: Ask Dr. Math: FAQ**
mathforum.org/dr.math/faq/faq.roman.html

**Quia—Matching, Flashcards, Concentration, Word Search**
www.quia.com/jg/66123.html

**Addition—Roman Numerals**
www.aaamath.com/add28y-add-roman.html

**Mathematics 1–2–3 number sense**
www.ucs.mun.ca/~rosalynb/numbersense.html

**Number Sense**
http://www.theteacherscorner.net/math/numbersense/index.htm

**Counting**
http://www.theteacherscorner.net/math/counting/index.htm

**Counting**
http://www.aaamath.com/B/cnt.htm

**Place Value**
http://www.aaamath.com/B/plc.htm

■ ■ ■ ■ ■

# CHAPTER 4

# WHOLE NUMBER OPERATIONS

There are four basic operations that the student must understand—addition, subtraction, multiplication, and division. This chapter will review the procedures for using these operations with whole numbers. Using the operations with rational numbers will be discussed in Chapter 5.

## ADDITION

Addition is the process of joining two or more sets together, and it is the most simple of the operations. Sometimes addition is taught by rote, where the addends (numbers that are added to one another to make a sum) and sums are memorized. Memorization, or automatic responses, is often the goal of simple addition, because immediate answers will facilitate mental arithmetic and work with multi-digit addends.

### Basic Facts

When a single digit whole number is added to another single digit whole number, the result is a basic fact. The basic facts are often written in an addition table. In this table the addends are written in the top horizontal column and the left vertical row. The cell in which the row and column intersect is the sum of the two addends. There are 100 basic facts for addition. As illustrated in the table below, it is obvious that the values above the diagonal (that runs from the top left to the bottom right) are mirrored by the values below the diagonal.

**Addition Table**

| + | 0 | 1 | 2 | 3 | 4 | 5 | 6 | 7 | 8 | 9 |
|---|---|---|---|---|---|---|---|---|---|---|
| 0 | 0 | 1 | 2 | 3 | 4 | 5 | 6 | 7 | 8 | 9 |
| 1 | 1 | 2 | 3 | 4 | 5 | 6 | 7 | 8 | 9 | 10 |
| 2 | 2 | 3 | 4 | 5 | 6 | 7 | 8 | 9 | 10 | 11 |
| 3 | 3 | 4 | 5 | 6 | 7 | 8 | 9 | 10 | 11 | 12 |
| 4 | 4 | 5 | 6 | 7 | 8 | 9 | 10 | 11 | 12 | 13 |
| 5 | 5 | 6 | 7 | 8 | 9 | 10 | 11 | 12 | 13 | 14 |
| 6 | 6 | 7 | 8 | 9 | 10 | 11 | 12 | 13 | 14 | 15 |
| 7 | 7 | 8 | 9 | 10 | 11 | 12 | 13 | 14 | 15 | 16 |
| 8 | 8 | 9 | 10 | 11 | 12 | 13 | 14 | 15 | 16 | 17 |
| 9 | 9 | 10 | 11 | 12 | 13 | 14 | 15 | 16 | 17 | 18 |

The basic facts for addition also have related basic subtraction facts. When one of the addends of a basic fact is subtracted from the sum, the resulting subtraction problem is known as a basic subtraction fact. For example, for the addition basic fact $7 + 8 = 15$, the related subtraction facts are $15 - 7 = 8$ and $15 - 8 = 7$. The two subtraction facts are also basic facts.

## Fact Families

Fact families are four related basic addition and subtraction facts. An example of a fact family would be:

$6 + 9 = 15$

$9 + 6 = 15$

$15 - 9 = 6$

$15 - 6 = 9$

Sometimes fact families are taught because the connections between the related facts facilitate memorization of the problems. Additionally, fact families are an example of the commutative property of addition.

## Properties

There are several distinctive characteristics known in the math world as "properties" of operations that are important to understand. It is not the ability to name the properties that is important, but the ability to understand the numbers and operations involved and, therefore, to understand the results that matters.

## Identity Property of Addition

Zero is the additive identity element. This is the element that, no matter what number it is added to, the answer is the number itself. Below are examples of the additive identity element:

$5 + 0 = 5$

$2 + 0 = 2$

$0 + 12 = 12.$

## Commutative Property of Addition

The commutative property of addition states that the addends may occur in any order and the sum does not change. Examples of the commutative property of addition are:

$5 + 4 = 9$ and $4 + 5 = 9$

$12 + 7 = 19$ and $7 + 12 = 19$

## Associative Property of Addition

The associative property of addition states that no matter how multiple addends are grouped, the sum will always be the same. An example of the associative property of addition is:

$(3 + 4) + 5 = 12$

$7 + 5 = 12$

$3 + (4 + 5) = 12$

$3 + 9 = 12$

The associative property also allows the matching of compatible numbers—numbers that add easily to sums that are easy to work with, such as ten. For example, when adding $3 + 4 + 5 + 6 + 7$, the 3 and 7 and the 4 and 6 can easily be combined to add to 10, thus making it easier to recognize that the sum of these addends is 25. It should be noted that the commutative property, as well as the associative property, allows such combining. The associative property does not allow changing the order of the numbers, it only allows changing the order in which the operation is performed. Combining the two properties allows rearranging multiple numbers as desired.

## SUBTRACTION

Subtraction is the inverse (opposite) of addition. The operations of addition and subtraction are sometimes taught as opposites, as with fact families. However, the student does not always make the connection between the two operations. Thinking of subtraction as completely separate from addition takes away the natural connection that exists. Understanding the operation and its connections to other mathematical concepts will facilitate deeper mathematical understanding.

Aside from the standard algorithm, subtraction problems or subtraction situations can be thought of in three main formats: take away, comparison, and missing addend (also known as "additive subtraction").

### Take Away

The following is an example of a "take away" problem: "Jamie has 22 pieces of bubble gum. She gives 5 pieces to Joe. How many pieces of gum does Jamie have left?" Take away problems are often the first type of subtraction that students learn. In this situation, a set of objects is taken away from another set and the quantity that is left is the solution (in subtraction, the solution or the answer is called the "difference"). Take away problems are the first type of subtraction encountered because they are easily modeled with concrete objects.

### Comparison

"Sarah has 12 pieces of bubble gum and Terri has 18 pieces. How many more pieces of bubble gum does Terri have than Sarah?" The difference in comparison problems answers the questions, "How many more?" or "How much less?". This difference is achieved through subtraction.

## Missing Addend

"If Maria has 5 pieces of bubble gum and she wants to give a piece to each of her 20 classmates, how many more pieces of gum does she need?" This type of problem, with a missing addend, is the most difficult to recognize as subtraction. It often asks how much more is needed to reach a specified quantity. When first learning to solve these problems, students may count on to see what it takes to get from the smaller value to the larger. However, this value is the difference between the two quantities, making this a subtraction problem.

## Addition and Subtraction with Regrouping

It is probably not necessary to review the common rules or algorithms for addition and subtraction, since it is an assumption that by reaching this level of study, a student has learned to add and subtract.

At this point it is important to interject a few points about algorithms. An "algorithm" is a series of rules or steps that is used to solve an equation. Our number system has a standard algorithm for each of the four operations. For example:

$$
\begin{array}{r}
1 \\
408 \\
+284 \\
\hline
692
\end{array}
$$

In the above problem, 408 plus 284, the standard algorithm says that the student should first combine the numbers in the ones place (8 + 4). Then, since this sum is greater than ten, the student should write the number of ones in the solution (2) and carry the 10. This is written as a 1 above the tens column. Then, the tens are added (0 + 8 + the 10 that was carried) and the sum (9 tens) written below the tens column. Next, the hundreds are added (4 + 2) and the sum (6 hundreds) is written below the hundreds column. The resulting sum is the solution of the problem. It is rare that the act of carrying is ever described as a mathematical action; however, this is what it is. In the above problem, when 8 and 4 are added to equal 12, the student is able to make one group of 10 out of 12 and this one group is what is marked in the tens column. The ones (2 of them) that are left out of the group of ten are the ones that appear in the sum. Many components, as noted, make up this standard algorithm, and yet often are left unmentioned. It is, therefore, necessary to emphasize the process and underlying understanding.

Just because a standard algorithm is the one that is typically taught to students, it does not mean there is only one way to reach the solution. There are often many alternative algorithms. Some of these alternative algorithms are taught in different cultures and countries. Others are developed through individual inventiveness. One alternative for the previous problem follows:

```
 408
+284
  12
  80
 600
 692
```

In this algorithm, the values of the numbers in each of the places (12 ones, 8 tens, and 6 hundreds) is added, the result is placed in the solution, and the partial sums are then added together. The result is the same, but it is arrived at by a different algorithm.

The significance of the alternative algorithms is not in knowing what each of them is and in being able to use each to solve problems, but instead to understand that they exist and that their use in solving problems is in no way incorrect. Understanding the way in which the alternative algorithm was constructed will determine if it is an acceptable way of reaching the solution.

## MULTIPLICATION

The basic multiplication facts are similar to the basic addition facts. They are the product of any two single digit "factors" (a factor is one of two or more numbers which, when multiplied together, produce a given "product," also known as the answer). These multiplication facts are often learned through rote memorization, often with flash cards. The basic meaning of multiplication is that of repeated addition or multiple groups. If one has 5 groups with 8 elements in each group the product of multiplying 5 times 8 (which is 40) is the sum of all of the elements in all of the groups: either 8 groups of 5 ($5 + 5 + 5 + 5 + 5 + 5 + 5 + 5 = 40$) or 5 groups of 8 ($8 + 8 + 8 + 8 + 8 = 40$).

**Multiplication Table**

| x | 0 | 1 | 2 | 3 | 4 | 5 | 6 | 7 | 8 | 9 |
|---|---|---|---|---|---|---|---|---|---|---|
| 0 | 0 | 0 | 0 | 0 | 0 | 0 | 0 | 0 | 0 | 0 |
| 1 | 0 | 1 | 2 | 3 | 4 | 5 | 6 | 7 | 8 | 9 |
| 2 | 0 | 2 | 4 | 6 | 8 | 10 | 12 | 14 | 16 | 18 |
| 3 | 0 | 3 | 6 | 9 | 12 | 15 | 18 | 21 | 24 | 27 |
| 4 | 0 | 4 | 8 | 12 | 16 | 20 | 24 | 28 | 32 | 36 |
| 5 | 0 | 5 | 10 | 15 | 20 | 25 | 30 | 35 | 40 | 45 |
| 6 | 0 | 6 | 12 | 18 | 24 | 30 | 36 | 42 | 48 | 56 |
| 7 | 0 | 7 | 14 | 21 | 28 | 35 | 42 | 49 | 56 | 63 |
| 8 | 0 | 8 | 16 | 24 | 32 | 40 | 48 | 56 | 64 | 72 |
| 9 | 0 | 9 | 18 | 27 | 36 | 45 | 54 | 63 | 72 | 81 |

There are also patterns that exist within the table of multiplication facts; however, these patterns are not the same as those that appear within the addition table. In the multiplication table, the diagonal that runs from the top left to the bottom right is the "line of reflection". The table above this line is reflected into the table below this line. There is a pattern in the line of reflection that shows that if a student begins with the first value in that diagonal, which is 0, and then adds consecutive odd numbers, he or she will reach each successive value in the diagonal, starting with one as in $0 + 1 = 1$, and then $1 + 3 = 4$, and $4 + 5 = 9$, and so on. Each horizontal or vertical column also has a pattern of adding successive groups of a value. For example, $0 + 3 = 3$, $3 + 3 = 6$, $6 + 3 = 9$, and so on. This pattern shows the connection between multiplication and repeated addition. The patterns may also be more complex. Examine any square of four entries, for example:

10   15

12   18

Note that the sum of the diagonal, $10 + 18$, is always one more than the sum of the other diagonal, $12 + 15$.

## Properties of Multiplication

Just as there were special properties for addition, there are also special properties for multiplication.

**Multiplicative Identity Property.** As evidenced in the multiplication table, the multiplicative identity element is one, meaning that any number multiplied by one yields the number itself, for example:

$5 \times 1 = 5$ or $1 \times 253 = 253$

**Multiplication by Zero.** Another special relationship is the one that exists when zero is one of the factors. Zero times any number gives a product of zero. The meaning for multiplication makes this obvious, since zero groups of five and five groups of zero both equal zero.

$5 \times 0 = 0$

$0 \times 5 = 0$

**Commutative Property of Multiplication.** Just as with addition, the commutative property states that the order of the factors does not matter.

$4 \times 5 = 9$ and $5 \times 4 = 9$

$3 \times 12 = 36$ and $12 \times 3 = 36$

**Associative Property of Multiplication.** The associative property of multiplication shows that the grouping when multiplying multiple factors does not affect the product.

$(3 \times 4) \times 5 =$ $\qquad$ $3 \times (4 \times 5) =$

$12 \times 5 = 60$ $\qquad$ $3 \times 20 = 60$

**Distributive Property of Multiplication.** The distributive property combines multiplication and addition. Writing

$3 \times (4 + 5) = 3 \times 9 = 27$

is the same as writing

$3 \times (4 + 5) = (3 \times 4) + (3 \times 5) = 12 + 15 = 27.$

Either the addition may be done first and then multiplied, or each of the numbers may be multiplied and the resulting products added together. Either way, the solution is the same.

**Two Types of Problems.**    Other than repeated addition, there are two other types of multiplication problems. The first is an area problem, where the measurements of a rectangle are given and the product is the area the rectangle covers. A second type of multiplication problem is a combination problem. An example of this type is "If I have four shirts and five pair of pants, how many different outfits do I have?". The solution is the result of a table or "Cartesian product" that includes all possible combinations. It is the product of the factors, meaning that the number of combinations is equal to the number of shirts times the number of shorts, 4 (shirts) × 5 (pants) = 20 possible outfits.

**Combination Table**

|  | WHITE | BLACK | BLUE | BROWN | GRAY |
|---|---|---|---|---|---|
| RED | red, white | red, black | red, blue | red, brown | red, gray |
| WHITE | white, white | white, black | white, blue | white, brown | white, gray |
| BLUE | blue, white | blue, black | blue, blue | blue, brown | blue, gray |
| BLACK | black, white | black, black | black, blue | black, brown | black, gray |

**Exponents.**    Exponents are a special situation in which multiplication is used. A number with an exponent (a symbol placed above and after another symbol to denote the number of times the latter is to be multiplied by itself) consists of two parts—the base and the exponent. The value is found when the base is multiplied by itself a number of times equal to the exponent. For example,

$3^4 = 3 \times 3 \times 3 \times 3 = 81.$

This problem shows that three is multiplied by itself four times.

## DIVISION

As addition and subtraction are inverse operations, so are multiplication and division. Division undoes the act of multiplication. Also, division can be thought of as repeated subtraction, thus connecting division and subtraction. There are two main types of division problems, partitioning and measurement.

## Partitioning

In a partitioning situation, one knows the number of sets and wants to know how many are in each set. For example, "I have 54 party favors and want to share them equally between my six friends. How many favors will each friend receive?" This type of division is also known as fair-sharing, because the action of sharing is common in modeling a solution. A solid understanding of partitioning is essential to understanding fractions as well.

## Measurement

The measurement situation models repeated subtraction. It seeks to answer the question, "How many groups are there?" For example, "I have 54 party favors and I want to give six of them to each of my guests. How many guests may I invite to the party?"

54 – 6 = 48 (that is one guest)

48 – 6 = 42 (that is a second guest)

42 – 6 = 36 (that is a third guest)

This process continues until groups of six can no longer be made. The number of groups is how many guests can be invited, or the quotient (answer) to the problem of 54 divided by 6.

## Division with Remainders

Not all division problems have even solutions where the dividend (the number being divided) is a multiple of the divisor (the number doing the dividing), and therefore there is no remainder. In fact, problems that occur naturally almost never have such solutions. In these situations, the procedure followed is the same, and because the amount left over must be smaller than the divisor, this leftover number is the remainder. The remainder may be written with an "r," which stands for remainder, or written as a fraction of the divisor (see Chapter 5).

## Division by Zero

Division by zero is "undefined," meaning that the answer cannot be determined, nor does it make sense. However, this statement does not mean that the quotient equals zero. Thinking of division by zero in light of the meaning of measurement or partitioning makes sense—if the problem asks for the quotient of 12/0, in terms of measurement the problem is asking how many groups of 0 can be measured from 12. In terms of partitioning, the problem is asking how to partition 12 items equally among 0 groups. Neither interpretation yields a comprehensible situation, and, therefore, division by zero is undefined.

## ORDER OF OPERATIONS

When solving a number sentence with more than one operation included, the student will find that rules exist for which operation to do first, which to do second, and so on. This order of operations is often remembered using the mnemonic phrase "Please Excuse My Dear Aunt Sally," where the first letter of each word stands for the operation—parenthesis, exponents, multiplication, division, addition, and subtraction. Done correctly, the operations are completed in order, from left to right in an equation. An example of the importance of order of operations is shown here:

$$3 \times 5 + 8 \div 2 = 15 + 4 = 19$$

The multiplication and division must be done before the addition. A common error for this number sentence is to solve it from left to right or $15 + 8 \div 2 = 23 \div 2 = 11.5$, which is not the correct answer. Another example of using order of operations to get the solution to a problem follows:

$$2 ( 3 + 4^2 / 2 - 1) =$$

$$2 ( 3 + 16 / 2 - 1) =$$

$$2 ( 3 + 8 - 1) =$$

$$2 ( 11 - 1) =$$

$$2 (10) =$$

20

The operations inside the parentheses occur first, with exponents being the first step followed by division from left to right, then the addition and subtraction left to right is done, and finally the multiplication outside the parenthesis. Without a specified order of operations, the same numerical sentence could result in multiple solutions.

## READINGS FOR STUDENTS

Anno, M. and Anno, M. (1983). *Anno's Mysterious Multiplying Jar.* New York: Philomel Books.

Burningham, J. (1983). *Pigs Plus.* New York: Viking Press.

Clemson, D. and Clemson, W. (2001). *My First Math Book.* New York: DK Publishing.

Daniels, T. and Bush, T. (2001). *Math Man.* New York: Orchard Books.

Dinio-Durkin, C. (1999). *Hickory Dickory Math (Grades K–1).* New York: Scholastic.

Dunn, P. and Vincent, B. L. (1988). *How Many?* New York: Random House.

Friedman, A. (1994). *The King's Commissioners.* Sausalito, CA: Marilyn Burns Education Associates.

Froman, R. and Fiammenghi, G. (1978). *The Greatest Guessing Game: A Book about Dividing.* New York: Thomas Y. Crowell Publishers.

Hawkins, C. (1983). *Adding Animals.* New York: G. P. Putnam's Sons.

Hawkins, C. (1984). *Take Away Monsters.* New York: G. P. Putnam's Sons.

Hutchins, P. (1986). *The Doorbell Rang.* New York: Greenwillow Books.

Koch, M. (1989). *Just One More.* New York: Greenwillow Books.

Leedy, L. (1997). *Mission: Addition.* New York: Holiday House.

Leedy, L. (2002). *Subtraction Action.* New York: Holiday House.

Liataud, J. (1999). *Times Tables the Fun Way: Book for Kids: A Picture Method of Learning the Multiplication Facts.* Minneapolis, MN: City Creek Press.

Long, L. (2000). *Dazzling Division: Games and Activities That Make Math Easy and Fun.* New York: John Wiley and Sons.

Long, L. (2000). *Marvelous Multiplication.* New York: John Wiley and Sons.

Long, L. (1996). *Domino Addition.* Watertown, MA: Charlesbridge Publishing.

Mathews, L. and Basset, J. (1978). *Bunches and Bunches of Bunnies.* New York: Scholastic.

McGrath, B. B. (1999). *More M & M's Brand Chocolate Candies Math.* Watertown, MA: Charlesbridge Publishing.

Moerbeck, K. and Dijs, C. (1988). *Six Brave Explorers.* Los Angeles: Price Stern Sloan.

Murphy, S. and Ulrich, G. (1997). *Divide and Ride (Mathstart).* Glenview, IL: Scott Foresman.

Napoli, D. J., Tchen, R., and Walrod, A. (2001). *How Hungry are You?* New York: Atheneum.

Neuschwander, C. (1998). *Amanda Bean's Amazing Dream.* New York: Scholastic.

Pallota, J. and Bolster, R. (2001). *The Hershey's Kisses Addition Book.* New York: Cartwheel Books.

Pallota, J. and Bolster, R. (2002). *The Hershey's Milk Chocolate Multiplication Book.* New York: Cartwheel Books.

Pappas, T. (1997). *The Adventures of Penrose the Mathematical Cat.* San Carlos, CA: Wide World Publishing/Tetra.

Peterson, I. and Henderson, N. (2000). *Math Trek 2: A Mathematical Space Odyssey.* New York: John Wiley and Sons.

Pinczes, E. (1995). *A Remainder of One.* Boston: Houghton Mifflin.

Pinczes, E. J. and Mackain, B. (1993). *One Hundred Hungry Ants.* New York: Houghton Mifflin.

Rocklin, J. (1997). *One Hungry Cat (Hello Math Reader. Level 3).* New York: Scholastic.

Trivett, J. V. and Maestro, G. (1975). *Building Tables on Tables: A Book about Multiplication.* New York: Thomas Y. Crowell Publishers.

## WEBSITES

**Operations**
www.theteacherscorner.net/math/operations/index.htm

**Addition**
www.aaamath.com/B/add.htm

**Subtraction**
www.aaamath.com/B/sub.htm

**Multiplication**
www.aaamath.com/B/mul.htm

**Division**
www.aaamath.com/B/div.htm

**Properties/relationships**
www.aaamath.com/B/pro.htm

**The Math Forum—Math Library—Basic Operations**
mathforum.org/library/topics/basic_ops/

**Basic Operations**
cne.gmu.edu/modules/dau/calculus/ functions/fbo_bdy.html

**Basic Math Operations**
www.aaamath.com/add53-alloper.html

**The GNU C Library**
www.gnu.org/manual/glibc-2.2.5/html_node/ Infinity-and-NaN.html

**Abacus Instruction—Sigma Educational Supply Co.**
www.citivu.com/usa/sigmaed/

**Mathematics**
www.scils.rutgers.edu/~ssaba/ resources/Mathematics99.html

**Addition**
www.aaamath.com/add.html

**Addition and Subtraction Game—An AskERIC Lesson Plan**
www.askeric.org/Virtual/Lessons/MathematicsArithmetic/ATH0002.html

**Subtraction**
www.aaamath.com/B/sub.htm

**Surfing the Net with Kids: Subtraction Flashcards**
www.surfnetkids.com/games/subtraction-fc.htm

**Teach ALL Students the Multiplication Facts**
www.multiplication.com/

**Math Forum: Multiplication Tips**
mathforum.org/k12/mathtips/multiplication.tips.html

**Multiplication Table**
www.math2.org/math/general/multiplytable.htm

**Multiplication Table Applet**
www.netrover.com/~kingskid/MulTab/Applet.html

**Interactive Internet Games**
www.multiplication.com/interactive_games.htm

**Cartoon Math**
www.cartoonmath.com/

**Multiplication Table**
www.allmath.com/Multtable.asp

**Multiplication Game**
quizhub.com/quiz/f-multiplication.cfm

**Quia—Matching**
www.quia.com/mc/66145.html

**Mrs. Wahl's Math Page**
www.chariho.k12.ri.us/ric/jwahl/wahlmath.htm

**JosseyBass: 190 Ready-to-Use Activities That Make Math Fun!**
www.josseybass.com/cda/product/0,,0787965855,00.html

**MegaMath**
www.bonus.com/bonus/card/megamath.html

# CHAPTER 5

# FRACTIONS, DECIMALS, AND PERCENTS

Rational numbers are numbers that can be expressed exactly by a ratio of two integers, i.e., "fractions" or the set of numbers that may be written as $\frac{a}{b}$, where $a$ and $b$ are whole numbers and $b$ is not equal to zero. A rational number can be any value, at any point, on a number line (although approximate values such as the square root of two are usually placed on a number line, their values are not exact and, therefore, not rational). Formal learning of rational numbers occurs as early as kindergarten with unit fractions of ½, ⅓, and ¼. Informal learning of these fractions may begin even younger, as children, for example, divide candy bars in half or share drinks. In spite of this early exposure, it is not uncommon for high school students, as well as many adults, to lack a thorough understanding of fractions. It is not surprising that many people have little more than a superficial recollection of what fractions are all about. Compared to the amount of time spent learning whole numbers, the time devoted to development and understanding of rational numbers is grossly inadequate. There is, however, a lot of motivation to understand and operate with rational numbers, because the natural occurrence of numbers in the world is not limited to those that are whole.

## MEANINGS OF FRACTIONS

It is important that a person who would like to be proficient in math understands what a fraction means. The meaning is not just the fractional notation, but the various types of models that a fraction can represent. Chapter 3 (Number Concepts) mentions that rational numbers encompass all of the values of the number line, not only the whole numbers, but the spaces between all of these whole numbers.

Translating this to other representations, there are three situations fractions can define: part-whole, ratio, and quotient.

## Part-Whole

The part-whole meaning for fractions is the most common one encountered. In this situation, there is a whole and the student is referring to a part of the whole. With this meaning, the numerator (top number of the fraction) represents the part, and the denominator (bottom number of the fraction) represents the whole. Use the following rectangle as an example:

With the rectangle above divided into five equal parts, ⅗ of the rectangle is shaded, because three of the five parts that make up the whole are shaded. Likewise, ⅖ of the rectangle is not.

## Ratio

In a ratio model, the fraction represents a ratio which compares two quantities to one another. For example, the number of tops a student has, compared to the number of jeans a student has is 12 to 4 or ¹²⁄₄. With this fraction, the student compares one quantity to another. This representation of fraction is very different from the part-whole representation. Because ratios are essentially one comparison, they cannot be added like part-whole fractions. It is important to understand that the fractional notation of numerator over denominator does not determine the meaning of the symbol, but it is determined by the situation from which it arises.

## Quotient

A third situation that may be written as a fraction is that of a division problem or quotient. If a student divides 12 by 4, the problem may be written as ¹²⁄₄. Thus, if this fraction is simplified, it is the quotient (answer) of 12 and 4, so it is 3.

## Partitioning

The concept of partitioning was mentioned in Chapter 4 (Whole Number Operations). A complete understanding of partitioning is essential to understanding fractions. To partition something means to separate it into equal parts. Together, the parts comprise a whole. Identifying the whole must be done in order to identify the number of parts the whole is separated, or partitioned, into.

## Part-Whole Models

Given that the part-whole model is the most commonly taught meaning for fractions, it is the one students, and adults, are most familiar with. There are three representations that can be used for a part-whole meaning: set, length, and area models.

**Set.** The set model is often difficult for young children to understand. With a set model, a group of objects is identified as the whole. For example, the student may have five pieces of candy in a bag. The five pieces make up the whole. If the student gives the teacher three pieces of candy, the student has given up ⅗ of the whole.

It is not this situation that causes the most difficulty with the set model. Rather, it is the situations in which the objects in the set are not the same size or shape that cause misconceptions. For example, Jesse has 12 toys in his toy box. Among the toys are a couple of balls, some toy trucks, a stuffed animal, and a coloring book. Not all of the toys are the same size and shape, but they are all an equivalent fraction of the set.

At a young age, a person often thinks about fractions as being equivalent parts of a set and assumes that means the parts are the same size. As shown in this example, that is not true with the set model. The set model may also lead to difficulty when modeling adding and subtracting. If ⅓ and ⅓ are added using a set model, the student may diagram ⅓ as shown below:

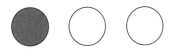

The common error is to combine the above diagram with another diagram that is identical, showing ⅓ + ⅓ as equal to ²⁄₆, which is incorrect:

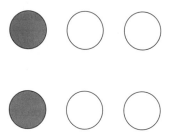

Instead, the correct way to approach this problem is to think of the set of three circles as one whole. So ⅓ of the set is the one shaded circle. When ⅓ is added to ⅓, the shaded circle is combined with another shaded circle, and these two are compared to the original whole, the set of three circles, as shown below. Thus, ⅓ + ⅓ = ²⁄₃.

**Length.**    The length model of a part-whole fraction is one that is used in both daily life and mathematical situations. In this model, the whole is a given length and the part is a fraction of that length. The most common example of this model is the use of a ruler and measurement. The mathematical situation occurs through one of the earliest models taught in mathematics, the number line. Once again, a given distance on the number line represents the whole and the part is a fraction of that distance. Only varying slightly in meaning, the number line is not used as a measuring device, but rather as a device that allows the student to record the location of values for further operation with them. For example, ¼ + ¼ + ¼ may be modeled on a number line:

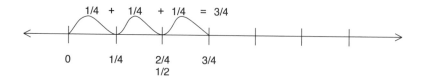

In this example, the whole is the distance from zero to one and the part is ¼ or one of four equal parts of that distance. These parts are added together to determine the sum.

**Region and Area.** The final example of part-whole models is area models, of which regions are a type. The region model of a part-whole fraction is the one learned in the earliest grades, and it is the model that most people remember and visualize. This model uses a geometric shape as the whole, usually a circle, square, or rectangle. Then, the whole is separated into congruent pieces, of equal size and shape. These are the parts. Two examples of region models are:

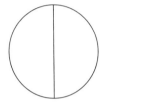 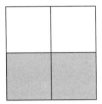

The area model is the broader category for a region model. Since the region model has parts that are congruent, the areas of the parts are equal. An area model is a shape in which the whole and the parts are shapes with equal areas, but not necessarily congruent. An example is the rectangle below. It is partitioned into three pieces of equal area and one of those three pieces is shaded, thus ⅓ is shaded. This model is the most difficult to understand.

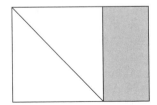

## OPERATIONS WITH FRACTIONS

### Addition

Addition of fractions has the same meaning as addition of whole numbers—it is the combining of two or more sets. The difference is that with fractions, the answer is always in relationship to an identified whole.

For example, ⅓ + ⅓ = ⅔. This meaning is that one third of a whole and one third of the same size whole may be combined to equal two thirds of that whole. Fractions whose numerators are one, as in the example above, are called "unit fractions." Unit fractions are usually the starting point for operations with fractions.

It is also important to understand the role of the denominator in the addition and subtraction of fractions. In the problem above, the denominator in both of the addends is three. This tells the student that he or she is combining units of the same size, which is essential knowledge.

The student cannot combine units of different sizes without first doing some adaptation, namely getting a common denominator. For example, ½ + ⅓ cannot be added without changing them to equivalent fractions.

### Equivalent Fractions

Equivalent fractions are two or more fractions whose values are equal to one another. For example, in the diagram below, ½ of the rectangle is shaded. This is the same amount as ¼ of the rectangle shaded. Using such a model makes it is easy to see that ½ and ¼ are equivalent:

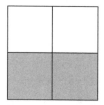

Unfortunately, it is not always convenient nor logical to determine the equivalent fractions through a drawing. Therefore, a particular algorithm (the set of rules or steps that are followed to solve a problem) is used. Following is an example using the two fractions, ¼ and ⅙. The first step is to identify a common denominator. Although any common multiple of 4 and 6 can be used, it is easiest to use the least common multiple. The least common multiple of 4 and 6 is 12. Twelve is the smallest multiple both 4 and 6 have in common.

$$\frac{1}{4} = \frac{}{12} \qquad \text{and} \qquad \frac{1}{6} = \frac{}{12}$$

The statements above can be read as "one-fourth equals some number of twelfths" and "one-sixth equals some number of twelfths." Since 12 is a multiple of 4, how many 4s equal 12? Regular multiplication shows that the answer is three. One-fourth, then, is converted to an equivalent fraction, with a denominator of 12, by multiplying it by three thirds, ⅗. The same procedure (in this case multiplying ⅙ by ²⁄₂) is used to convert one-sixth to an equivalent fraction whose denominator is 12. See the two processes below:

$$\frac{1}{4} \times \frac{3}{3} = \frac{3}{12} \qquad \text{and} \qquad \frac{1}{6} \times \frac{2}{2} = \frac{2}{12}$$

It is important to note that in order to create equivalent fractions, the initial fractions were multiplied by a fraction whose numerator and denominator were the same value. Any fraction whose numerator and denominator is the same is equal to one, which is the multiplicative identity element—multiplying something by one does not change the value. The solution is the same as the factor that was multiplied by one. This solution does not change in the case of fractions. The solution appears in a different form, with different numerators and denominators, but the values of the two fractions are the same or equivalent.

Therefore, fractions with unlike denominators must first be changed into fractions with equivalent denominators before they may be added. For example:

$$\frac{1}{4} \times \frac{3}{3} = \frac{3}{12}$$

$$+$$

$$\frac{2}{3} \times \frac{4}{4} = \frac{8}{12}$$

Adding the two sets of twelfths gives the sum or answer of eleven twelfths:

$$\frac{3}{12} + \frac{8}{12} = \frac{11}{12}$$

There is also a connection that can be made here with measurement. In the above problem, the question can be asked, "If you combine three twelfths with eight twelfths, how many twelfths do you have?" The answer is eleven twelfths. So the student can think of twelfths, or the denominator, as the unit and the numerator as the quantity of those units. This situation is similar to adding 3 inches and 8 inches when 3 and 8 are the quantity of units the student is working with and inches are the units.

## Subtraction

The meanings for subtraction with fractions are the same as the meanings with whole numbers: fraction subtraction can be take away, comparison, or missing addend. Additionally, the operation of subtraction with fractions follows the same rules as the operation of addition. If the two fractions have a common denominator, the numerators are subtracted, as with whole numbers, and the difference is placed over the common denominator. If the denominators are not the same, equivalent fractions must be created so the denominators are the same and then the fractions are subtracted.

Two examples are given below. In the first, the denominators are the same, so simple subtraction is performed with the numerators:

$$
\begin{array}{r}
\frac{5}{6} \\
- \frac{1}{6} \\
\hline
\frac{4}{6}
\end{array}
$$

In this second example, the denominators are not the same, so they must be converted before the subtraction can be performed:

$$
\begin{array}{r}
\frac{2}{3} \times \frac{4}{4} = \frac{8}{12} \\
- \frac{1}{4} \times \frac{3}{3} = \frac{3}{12} \\
\hline
\end{array}
$$

Subtracting the two sets of twelfths gives the answer of five twelfths:

$$\frac{8}{12} - \frac{3}{12} = \frac{5}{12}$$

## Simplifying

Most textbooks and many teachers insist that solutions be written in "simplest form." This means that the numerator and denominator of a fraction have no common factor larger than one. The solution of ⁴⁄₆, in the first of the two problems above, is not in simplest form. The 4 and 6 have a common factor larger than one: that common factor is 2. Just as one is the multiplicative identity element, any number can also be divided by one, and it does not change the value. Therefore, to simplify ⁴⁄₆, the student can divide it by ²⁄₂, with both the numerator (4) and denominator (6) divided by 2. The equivalent fraction that results is:

$$\frac{4 \div 2}{6 \div 2} = \frac{2}{3} \quad \begin{array}{l}\text{(numerator)}\\\text{(denominator)}\end{array}$$

for a final answer of ²⁄₃. A solution that is not in simplest form is not incorrect, it is just not in the usually desired form.

## Improper Fractions and Mixed Numbers

Improper fractions are those whose numerators are larger than their denominators. For example, ¹¹⁄₃ and ⁵⁄₂ are both improper fractions. Improper fractions are always larger or smaller than one and negative one, respectively. Improper fractions can be changed into another form, that of a whole or mixed number. An improper fraction that can be changed into a whole number is ³⁄₁, which is equivalent to 3, and ⁸⁄₂, which if both the numerator and denominator are divided by 2, is equivalent to ⁴⁄₁, which is equivalent to 4.

If the denominator cannot be simplified to one, then the improper fraction can be converted to an equivalent mixed number. The numerator is divided by the denominator, and the resulting quotient is the whole number part of the mixed number. The remainder of the division problem is put into the numerator, over the initial denominator, making the fractional part of the mixed number. In the following example, the improper fraction is ¹⁵⁄₄.

Dividing 15 by 4 gives a whole number quotient (answer to a division problem) of 3 (since 4 divides 15 three times) and a remainder of 3. The answer, then, is ¹⁵⁄₄ = 3 and ¾.

In addition, it is expected that mixed numbers may need to be converted back to improper fractions for operation purposes. To do so, the denominator is multiplied by the whole number and the product is added to the numerator. In the example above, the denominator 4 is multiplied by the whole number 3, and then the 3 is added to the numerator (also 3, in this case). This sum becomes the numerator of the improper fraction and it is placed over the original denominator.

In another example, $4\frac{2}{5}$, the whole number 4 is multiplied by the denominator 5 to get a product (answer to multiplication problem) of 20, which is added to the numerator 2 for a total sum of 22 as the numerator. That numerator is presented over the same denominator, which is still 5:

$$4\frac{2}{5} = \frac{22}{5}$$

When the student is faced with operations with improper fractions, those fractions should be acted upon in the same as proper fractions, and the solution should be converted to a mixed number. Mixed numbers may be converted to improper fractions, the operation done, and the solution converted back to a mixed number.

## Multiplication

Unlike addition and subtraction, the meaning of multiplication with fractions is not always the same as the meaning of multiplication with whole numbers. An example of a case in which it is the same is in the problem $3 \times \frac{1}{4}$. The problem is, "What is three groups of one-fourth equal to?" In this case, repeated addition would be appropriate to think about the solution. Three groups of one-fourth equals $\frac{1}{4} + \frac{1}{4} + \frac{1}{4}$ = ¾. When the student is thinking about this problem in terms of an algorithm, the three, when written as a fraction, is written as ³⁄₁. The numerators of the two factors are multiplied, as are the denominators of the two factors.

$\frac{3}{1} \times \frac{1}{4} = \frac{3 \times 1}{1 \times 4} = \frac{3}{4}$, so the final product is ¾.

If the fraction is the first factor, the meaning of the problem changes, in spite of the fact that the algorithm remains the same. An example of this second type of problem is $\frac{1}{4} \times \frac{2}{3}$. Multiplying the numerators and denominators gives $1 \times 2$ over $4 \times 3 = \frac{2}{12}$. This can be simplified to ⅙. The meaning behind this problem is, "What is one-fourth of a group of two-thirds?" Explaining the problem further, if one has, for example, two-thirds of a cup of sugar and needs one-fourth of that amount to make some cookies, what fraction of a cup is needed to make the cookies? The whole for the solution is the same that was used to determine two-thirds: a cup. The one-fourth does not refer to this whole, but instead refers to a portion of the two-thirds.

Similarly, a fraction times a fraction uses the same meaning to find a fractional part of another fraction and relate it back to an identified whole. Meanwhile, the algorithm does not change. For example:

$$\frac{2}{3} \times \frac{1}{5} = \frac{2\times1}{3\times5} = \frac{2}{15}$$

*Canceling.* Often, the strategy of canceling is taught to assist in multiplication. In this procedure, factors that are common to the numerator and the denominator are divided from each prior to the multiplication. This is not an algorithm, but a strategy to assist with simplifying. Below is an example of canceling:

$$\frac{4}{5} \times \frac{10}{12} = \frac{2}{5} \times \frac{10}{6} = \frac{1}{5} \times \frac{10}{3} = \frac{1}{1} \times \frac{2}{3} = \frac{2}{3}$$

In this procedure the 4 and the 12 in the first portion of the problem have a common factor of 2. So, 4 and 12 are each divided by two, making the resulting problem ⅖ × ¹⁰⁄₆. Then, since 2 and 6 still have 2 as a common factor, they were again each divided by 2, resulting in ⅕ × ¹⁰⁄₃. Finally, the 5 and the 10 have 5 as a common factor, so dividing each of the terms by 5 leaves ¹⁄₁ × ⅔ which multiplies to equal ⅔.

It is important to note two things about canceling. First, ¹⁄₁ × ⅔ is not the same problem as ⅘ × ¹⁰⁄₁₂. It does, however, take out the common factors. This means that simplifying occurs prior to the operation, rather than after it has been completed. Second, this procedure can only happen if there is a factor common to both a numerator and a denominator, since two numerators or two denominators may not be used.

## Division

The meaning of division of fractions is seldom taught, making it difficult to begin with an explanation of the problem. Therefore, this discussion will begin with the algorithm and then move back to where the discussion should have started—with an understanding of what is being asked.

The commonly taught algorithm for division of fractions is to invert the second fraction and then multiply. So, ½ divided by ⅔ = ½ × ³⁄₂ = ¾. The algorithm is easy enough to memorize, and once the student knows how to multiply, the final step is accomplished with no difficulty. It is important to note that only the second factor is inverted, and that inverting the first factor will result in an incorrect answer. Unfortunately, this knowledge does not help a student to understand what is being asked by the problem, nor does the knowledge enable the student to put the problem into a familiar context.

It is necessary to first understand the meaning of a division problem with fractions. The problem of ½ divided by ⅔ should be considered again. A helpful way to think about this problem is in relationship to the measurement meaning of division, and to put it into a particular situation, for example, measuring cups of sugar.

If both ½ and ⅔ are fractions of the same size whole (a cup), how many two-thirds of a cup can be measured from one-half cup? Or in a problem, "Henry wants to make cookies that call for ⅔ cup of sugar, but he only has ½ cup of sugar. Can he make a full batch of cookies? No. So how much or what fraction of a batch of cookies can he make?" Since the answer is less than one, the vocabulary can be changed to ask, "How much of a piece (or batch) equal to one-half may be measured (or made) using two-thirds?" The answer is that ¾ (of ⅔ of a cup) can be measured, or that ¾ of a batch can be made. The quotient is three-fourths of the two-thirds, not three-fourths of the whole cup, because two-thirds of a cup was what was needed to equal one full batch. The concept may be difficult at first to understand, but it is necessary in order to connect fraction division to the division occurring in the more familiar context of whole numbers.

## Decimals

Decimals are a representation of rational numbers based on powers of tens as the partitioning of the whole. For example, 0.5 is the same as ⁵⁄₁₀, and, in another example, 0.374 = 374/1000. All of the denominators are powers of ten. The effect on notation is that it carries the base ten system to the right of the decimal point, into fractional terms. This connection to fractions is significant in that the whole is a unit, or the length between zero and one. This whole is partitioned into ten equal parts. To further separate this unit into hundredths, each of the ten parts are further partitioned into ten more equal parts. The more places that exist to the right of the decimal point, the more this process is continued.

Operations with decimals are similar to operations with whole numbers, but there are a few important points to keep in mind. When adding and subtracting whole numbers, one must line up the decimal points. For example:

| 23.451 | 614.3 |
|--------|-------|
| +4.39  | −38.67 |
| 27.841 | 575.63 |

In the subtraction problem above, it is important to remember that 0.3 is the same as 0.30 and should be treated as such for the purpose of the algorithm.

With multiplication of decimals, the decimal points do not have to be lined up to complete the algorithm:

```
   3.457
 ×  2.6
 2 0742
 6 914
 8.9882
```

The difference between decimal and whole number multiplication is that the sum of the places to the right of the decimal point in the factors is determined, and that many places are shown to the right of the decimal point in the solution. Using the distributive property and an understanding of fraction multiplication, this makes sense. The product is the same as two groups of 3.457 plus six-tenths of a group of 3.457.

Division with decimals, where there are no values to the right of the decimal point in the divisor, follow the same algorithm as division using whole numbers. The exception is that the decimal point from the dividend is placed above the division sign to be at the appropriate place in the quotient. For example, the long division problem 23.68 divided by four would look as follows:

```
     5.92
  4 )23.68
     20
     36
     36
      8
      8
      0
```

If the divisor has digits to the right of the decimal point, the divisor is converted to a whole number. This is done by multiplying by an appropriate power of 10. So, 0.4 is multiplied by 10 to equal 4. Next, 3.45 is multiplied by 100 to equal 345. As a result of the divisor being multiplied by a power of 10, the dividend must also be multiplied by this same number. An example of this process is the problem 874.250 divided by 34.8, shown below:

$$
34.8\overline{)874.250} \quad \text{becomes the problem} \quad 348\overline{)8742.50}
$$

$$
\begin{array}{r}
24 \phantom{00} \\
348\overline{)8742.50} \\
\underline{704} \phantom{000} \\
1702 \phantom{00} \\
\underline{1392} \phantom{00} \\
310 \phantom{00}
\end{array}
$$

In order to move the decimal point in the divisor to the right, making 34.8 into the whole number 348, the decimal point in the dividend 874.250 must also move one place to the right, keeping the relationship proportional and making the dividend 8742.50. This act of moving the decimal point to the right has the same effect as multiplying by a multiple of ten.

## Percents

Percents are not actually an area of mathematics, but a notational representation. They are a way to represent fractions whose denominator is 100 or to represent decimals to the hundredth place. Because they are figured on powers of ten, they are easy and fun to work with.

Fractions may be converted to percents by dividing the numerator by the denominator and then multiplying the quotient by 100. An easy example follows:

$\frac{3}{4} = .75 = 75\%$

By contrast, a percent may be converted to a fraction by placing the percent over a denominator of 100 and then simplifying, as in the following example:

$8\% = \frac{8}{100} = \frac{2}{25}$.

Percents may also be converted to decimals. In these cases, the percent is divided by 100. The resulting quotient is the equivalent decimal, as in this example:

$43\% = 0.43$

Decimals may be converted to percents by following an inverse procedure—multiplying the decimal value by 100. The resulting product is a percent, as in this final example:

$4.56 = 456\%$

## READING FOR STUDENTS

Adler, D. A. and Tobin, N. (1997). *Fraction Fun*. New York: Holiday House.

Alexander, R. B., Robinson, T., Martin, C. and Saaveda, B. W. (2001). *Fraction Jugglers: Game and Work Book and Math Game Cards*. New York: Workman.

Bolster, R., McGrath, W., McGrath, B. B. and Mazzola, F. (2000). *The Cheerios Counting Book*. New York: Cartwheel Books.

Cummings, A. and Hamilton, L. (1998). *Painless Fractions*. Hauppage, NY: Barrons Painless Series.

Greenes, C., Dacy, L. S. and Spungin, R. (1999). *Fractions and Decimals: Grade 5*. Lebanon, IN: Pearson Learning.

Jaffe, E. D. (2002). *Can You Eat a Fraction?* Mankata, MN: Pebble Books.

Leedy, L. (1996). *Fraction Action*. Glenview, IL: Scott Foresman/Pearson.

Long, L. (2001). *Fabulous Fractions: Games, Puzzles, and Activities That Make Math Easy and Fun*. New York: John Wiley and Sons.

McGrath, B. B. and Glass, R. (2001). *Skittles Riddles Math*. Watertown, MA: Charlesbridge Publishing.

McMillan, B. (1991). *Eating Fractions*. New York: Scholastic.

Mitchell, C. (1999). *Funtastic Math! Decimals and Fractions: Grade 4–8*. New York: Scholastic.

Moncure, J. B. and Hohag, L. (1988). *How Many Ways Can You Cut a Pie?* Chicago: Children's Press.

Murphy, S. J. and Karas, G. B. (1996). *Give Me Half!* Glenview, IL: Scott Foresman/Pearson.

Murphy, S. J. and O'Malley, K. (1999). *Jump, Kangaroo, Jump!* New York: HarperTrophy.

Packard, E. (2001). *Little Numbers: and Pictures That Just Show How Little They Are*. Brookfield, CT: Millbrook Press.

Pallotta, J. and Bolster, R. (1999). *The Hershey's Milk Chocolate Bar Fractions Book*. New York: Cartwheel Books.

Pallotta, J. and Bolster, R. (2002). *Apple Fractions*. New York: Cartwheel Books.

Penner, L. R. and Billin-Frye, P. (2000). *Clean-Sweep Campers*. New York: Kane Press.

Pinczes, E. J. and Enos, R. (2001). *Inchworm and a Half*. New York: Houghton Mifflin.

Pistoia, S. and Court, R. (2002). *Fractions (Mighty Math)*. Chanhassen, NY: Child's World.

Ziefert, H. and Bolam, E. (1998). *Rabbit and Hare Divide an Apple*. New York: Puffin.

## WEBSITES

### Fractions
www.theteacherscorner.net/math/fractions/index.htm

**Decimals**
www.aaamath.com/B/dec.htm

**Percent**
www.aaamath.com/B/pct.htm

**Fractions**
www.aaamath.com/B/fra.htm

**Properties/relationships**
www.aaamath.com/B/pro.htm

**Simplifying Fractions**
www.aaamath.com/g8-66h-simpfrac.html

**Amby's Math Resources—Simplifying Fractions**
amby.com/educate/math/2-2_simp.html

**5–3 Simplifying Fractions**
www.free-ed.net/fr07/lfc/course070101_01/menu0503.htm

**The Four Mathematical Operations with Fractions**
web.buddyproject.org/web011/web011/

**The Four Mathematical Operations with Fractions**
web.buddyproject.org/web011/web011/subtract.htm

**Multiplying Decimals and Mixed Numbers**
www.shodor.org/interactivate/lessons/multdeci.html

**Skill in Arithmetic: The Meaning of Decimals**
www.themathpage.com/ARITH/decimals.htm

**Meaning of Decimals (tenths and hundredths)**
www.uwinnipeg.ca/~jameis/New%20Pages/EYR40.html

**Lesson Planet Math, Decimals Page**
lessonplanet.teacherwebtools.com/search/Math/Decimals/

**Primary 4 Mathematics**
www.tut-world.com/p4_maths.htm

**Mathematics—Grade 5**
www.op97.k12.il.us/instruct/cg/MATH.5.html

**Fractions**
www.aaamath.com/B/fra.htm

**Cynthia Lanius' Lessons: Fraction Shapes**
math.rice.edu/~lanius/Patterns/

**Fractions**
www.mathleague.com/help/fractions/fractions.htm

**Decimals**
www.aaamath.com/B/dec.htm

**Decimals Main Page**
pittsford.monroe.edu/jefferson/calfieri/decimals/decimalsmain.html

**Converting Decimals to Fractions**
www.sosmath.com/algebra/fraction/frac6/frac6.html

**Math, Fractions and Decimals!!!!**
www.blarg.net/~math/FDMENU.HTM

**Numbers—Multiplying Decimals—First Glance**
www.math.com/school/subject1/lessons/S1U1L5GL.html

**Percents and Ratios**
www.aaamath.com/B/pct.htm

**Percents**
www.iit.edu/~smile/ma9510.html

**Percents/Fractions/Decimals Review**
www.purplemath.com/modules/percents.htm

■ ■ ■ ■ ■

# CHAPTER 6

# ALGEBRAIC THINKING

Algebraic thinking involves identifying, representing, generalizing, and formalizing patterns. This type of reasoning is at the heart of mathematics. It begins with the earliest concept of numbers and continues to develop and expand throughout the curriculum.

## PATTERNS

### Repeating Patterns

Repeating patterns are studied and learned formally as early as kindergarten. Repeating patterns begin as visual, auditory, or tactile patterns. These patterns have a small core of elements that repeat themselves. Repeating patterns are often named using letters of the alphabet. An A B repeating pattern is the simplest type of repeating pattern. In this case the core has two elements, A and B. If the pattern is an auditory one, it might be clap, snap, clap, snap, and so on. If the pattern is a visual pattern, it might be square, circle, square, circle, and so on. Color is often used to model or color repeating patterns. Repeating patterns can also be written using numbers. For example, 1, 3, 5, 5, 1, 3, 5, 5, 1,...is an example of a numerical repeating pattern whose core is A B C C.

### Growing Patterns

Growing patterns, although present in some children's literature, are generally not studied in mathematics until fourth or fifth grade. Examples from children's literature include "The Twelve Days of Christmas" and "There Was an Old Lady Who Swallowed a Fly." The rhymes and the repetition make these patterns fun to recite as well as memorable. In mathematics, these types of patterns are called "sequences." Instead of looking for a repeating pattern, the student looks for an algebraic relationship that will tell what the pattern will be at any given point in the sequence. A couple of examples of repeating patterns are 1, 2, 4, 7, 11,…and 1, 4, 9, 16,….

In working with sequences, the initial goal is to look for the relationship that maps one element of the pattern to the next. Once this relationship has been identified, it is applied to determine the element that would come next. If this relationship works, it is then generalized to determine the value of any point in the sequence.

### Relationships

The description that tells how any pattern changes from a given frame, or element, to the next is called a "recursive relationship." So, in the pattern 1, 4, 9, 16, the relationship is that the elements are the squares of consecutive numbers (1, 2, 3, 4). Therefore, the next element in the pattern is 25 ( the square of 5). Actually, this is not the only relationship that exists in this pattern. Another pattern that can be identified is that consecutive odd numbers are added to each of the pattern values to reach the next. So, $1 + 3 = 4$, and $4 + 5 = 9$. The next value that would be added is 7. In fact, many patterns have multiple relationships. Any relationship that provides the solution is correct, and one is no more correct than another.

Once the relationship can be generalized into a rule—that when given the position in the sequence one is able to determine the value of the element in that position—the sequence is said to have a "functional relationship." In the pattern 1, 4, 9, 16, 25, it is easy to see from the pattern that the thirtieth element, for example, would be $30^2$ or 900.

### FUNCTIONS

The Principles and Standards for School Mathematics suggests that function concepts should focus on relationships in meaningful contexts and multiple methods of connecting these relationships. A "function" is a rule that connects two sets and uniquely associates elements of the first set with elements of the second set. The elements in the first set are known as "independent variables," while the elements in the second set are known as "dependent variables." The process of searching for the relationship that ties the first set to the second set is the attempt to search for a pattern, for order. This search is the process of doing mathematics.

Functional relationships may be found in patterns, as mentioned above. More importantly, functional relationships may be found in real world situations. By observing the many contexts of these relationships in real world situations, students begin to recognize them more easily. Additionally, mathematics is identified as something that exists in the world, rather than simply through using numerals and algorithms. Through real world situations, functions can be represented in three different formats: tables, graphs, and equations.

A discussion of the multiple representation of function can be examined, given the following problem: Mrs. Joseph buys boxes of pretzels for $5.00 for a box of 12 pretzels. She then sells the pretzels for 75 cents each. How much profit will she make on $n$ boxes of pretzels?

## Tables

From the data given above, a table can be constructed that pairs the number of pretzels sold with the amount of profit. For example:

| NUMBER OF PRETZELS SOLD | PROFIT |
|---|---|
| 1 | –4.25 |
| 2 | –3.50 |
| 3 | –2.75 |
| 4 | –2.00 |
| 5 | –1.25 |
| 6 | –.50 |
| 7 | .25 |
| 8 | 1.00 |
| 9 | 1.75 |
| 10 | 2.50 |
| 11 | 3.25 |
| 12 | 4.00 |

Mrs. Joseph makes four dollars profit on each box. Another table modeling this profit follows:

| NUMBER OF BOXES SOLD | PROFIT |
|---|---|
| 1 | 4.00 |
| 2 | 8.00 |
| 3 | 12.00 |
| 4 | 16.00 |
| n | 4n |

## Graphs

For this situation, a graph may also be made where the value on the x-axis is the number of boxes sold and the value on the y-axis is the amount of profit:

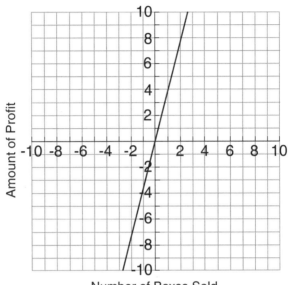

Number of Boxes Sold

A graph illustrates the values of x and y. These values are taken from the table, where in this case, the number of boxes sold is the x and the amount of profit is the y. The x and y values make a "coordinate pair," and connecting the multiple coordinate pairs makes the graph.

**Equations.** The generalized functional relationship for the previous problem's graph and table is $y = 4x$. This pairs the x and y values through the functional relationship. Thorough understandings of functions are built through a combination of tables, graphs, or equations.

## VARIABLES

A variable is a symbol that can stand for any one of a set of objects. Variables may be shapes such as squares or circles, which they are in the early grades. It is common to ask children what the box equals in $5 + \square = 8$. As the concept of variable is more formally taught, the box or circle is replaced by a letter. Initially this letter is usually *x* or *n*. The letter stands for a value, or in the case of a functional relationship, any one of a set of values. So, $5 + x = 8$ has the same meaning as $5 + \square = 8$.

## Variable Expressions

Variable expressions contain numbers and variables, but they do not contain equal signs. Therefore, variable expressions alone, without additional information, cannot be solved. Examples of variable expressions are $5x$ and $2b$. Variable expressions may also have operators, so they may be simplified. Having operators means that operations—such as addition, subtraction, multiplication, division, and exponents—may be present in variable expressions. The effect of their presence is that the variable expressions may be written in simpler form than they may initially appear. This situation occurs when terms that look alike, such as $2x$ and $3x$, may be combined. For example, $2 + 3x - 4 + 8x$ can be simplified to $-2 + 11x$, but until the expression has an equal sign or an inequality sign, it may not be solved. Another example is $5x + 2z - 4x + 7z$. The x terms and the z terms can be simplified so that the expression can be read as $x + 9z$.

## Variable Equations

A variable equation contains variables, an equal sign, and a quantity which the variables equal. With variable equations the goal is usually to find the value of the variable. The following is an example of a variable equation: $3x + 8x = 44$. The expression on the left side of the equation can simplified so the equation reads $11x = 44$. Then, using inverse operations, both sides of the equation are divided by 11 so that $x = 4$. This value for x may be tested by substituting it back into the original equation and solving to determine if the left side of the equation is equal to the right side.

## Inequalities

Inequalities are similar to equations; however, instead of an equal sign, there is a greater than, less than, greater than or equal to, or less than or equal to sign. Initial understanding of these signs should begin as part of number sense, when students learn to compare numbers.

## NUMBER THEORY

### Odds and Evens

One of the first number theory topics that a student encounters is classifying numbers as odd or even. This situation usually happens as a result of counting by even numbers, 2, 4, 6, 8, and so on. These numbers are identified as even, while the skipped numbers are identified as odd.

Modeling is also important to understanding odds and evens. If a set can be arranged so that each item in the set matches with another item in the set, then the set has an even number of elements. However, if the set has one item that can not be matched, the set has an odd number of elements. An example of this modeling:

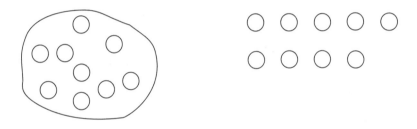

The circles in the set are matched in pairs. Since there is one circle that does not have a match, there is an odd number of circles.

### Factors, Composites and Primes

Another number theory topic encountered in the elementary grades is that of factors, composites, and primes. When two numbers are multiplied together, each of them is called a "factor."

In the problem $3 \times 7 = 21$, 3 and 7 are factors.

In the previous case, 21 is called a "multiple," because it is a multiple of 3 as well as a multiple of 7. Since 21 has factors (3 and 7) other than one and itself, it is a "composite number." Other examples of composite numbers are 325, 80, and 9, all of which have factors other than one and themselves. A number that has only two factors, one and itself (like 5, 17, and 41) is called a "prime number" (which means that 1 is neither a prime nor a composite number).

## Greatest Common Factor and Least Common Multiple

Given two or more numbers, it is sometimes necessary to find the "greatest common factor" or the "least common multiple." The greatest common factor is used when simplifying a fraction. The least common multiple may be used to find a common denominator for which each is a factor, to allow adding of two fractions. In such a case, the least common multiple is known as the least common denominator, or LCD.

The easiest way to find the greatest common factor of two numbers is to list the factors of each of the numbers, then identify the greatest factor they both have in common.

The most taught way to find the least common multiple is to list multiples of each of the numbers until a common multiple is found. Both of these methods are simple, with little calculation involved. Unfortunately, many confuse the greatest common factor with the least common multiple because of a failure to recall the difference between a factor and a multiple. Although there are other methods that can be used to find the values of the greatest common factor and least common multiple, the procedures explained here are the most straightforward and easy to understand.

**READINGS FOR STUDENTS**

Anno, M. (1989). *Anno's Math Games II.* New York: Philomel Books.

Burns, M. and Hairston, M. (1975). *The I Hate Mathematics! Book.* Boston: Little, Brown.

Burns, M. and Weston, M. (1982). *Math for Smarty Pants.* Boston: Little, Brown & Co.

Charosh, M. (1974). *Number Ideas Through Pictures.* New York: Thomas Y. Crowell Publishers.

Enzensberger, H. and Berner, R. S. (2000). *The Number Devil: A Mathematical Adventure.* New York: Metropolitan Books.

Fehr, H. (1965). *Number Patterns Make Sense: A Wise Owl Book.* New York: Holt, Rinehart & Winston.

Hayes, C. & Hayes, D. (1987). *Number Mysteries.* Milwaukee, WI: Penworthy Publishing.

Heath, R. V. (1953). *Mathemagic: Magic, Puzzles, and Games with Numbers.* New York: Dover Publications.

Juster, N. and Feiffer, J. (1993). *The Phantom Tollbooth.* New York: Random House.

Lee, M. (2001). *40 Fabulous Math Mysteries Kids Can't Resist.* New York: Scholastic.

Miranda, A. and Powell, P. (1999). *Monster Math.* New York: Harcourt.

Nagda, A. W. & Bickel, C. (2000). *Tiger Math: Learning to Graph from a Baby Tiger.* New York: Henry Holt.

Peterson, I. and Henderson, W. (1999). *Math Trek: Adventures in the Mathzone.* New York: John Wileyand Sons.

Pluckrose, H. (1995). *Time (Math Counts).* New York: Children's Press.

Schwartz, D. M. and Meisel, P. (1999). *On Beyond a Million: An Amazing Math Journey.* New York: Bantam Doubleday Dell.

Schwartz, D. M. and Moss, M. (1998). *G is for Googol: A Math Alphabet Book.* Berkeley, CA: Tricycle Press.

Srivastava, J. J. and Ehlert, L. (1979). *Number Families.* New York: Grosset & Dunlap.

Tang, G. and Briggs, H. (2001). *The Grapes of Math: Mind Stretching Math Riddles.* New York: Scholastic.

Weiss, C. and Corwin, J. (1976). *666 Jellybeans! All That? An Introduction to Algebra.* New York: Thomas Y. Crowell Publishers.

Zaslavsky, C. (1998). *Math Games & Activities from Around the World.* Chicago: Chicago Review Press.

## WEBSITES

**Algebra**
www.aaamath.com/B/alg.htm

**Integrated Lesson Plans**
faldo.atmos.uiuc.edu/WEATHER/weather.html

**Building Bridges to Algebraic Thinking**
illuminations.nctm.org/lessonplans/6-8/bridges/

**Electronic Resources—Developing Algebraic Thinking**
my.nctm.org/eresources/view_article.asp?article_id=2072

**Algebraic Thinking Series**
www.mathsolutions.com/mb/content/ publications/p_algethink.html

**Session 1: Algebraic Thinking**
www.learner.org/channel/courses/ learningmath/algebra/session1/

**Number Theory—from MathWorld**
mathworld.wolfram.com/topics/NumberTheory.html

**Mathematics Archives—Topics in Mathematics—Number Theory**
archives.math.utk.edu/topics/numberTheory.html

**11: Number Theory**
www.math.niu.edu/~rusin/known-math/index/11-XX.html

**Lessons on Number Theory from Math Goodies**
www.mathgoodies.com/lessons/toc_vol3.shtm

**I Love Binary, Primes, and Factors Page**
home.earthlink.net/~usondermann/binary.html

**Repunit Primes and Factors**
www.swox.com/gmp/repunit.html

**Educational Repository: Mathematics**
www.salinaok.com/edu/mathrepository.html

**Prime factors #1**
www.delphiforfun.org/Programs/PrimeFactors1.htm

**Grade 5: Primes and Composites**
www.uwinnipeg.ca/~jameis/New%20Pages/MYR20.html

**Recreational Mathematics Topics**
www.uwgb.edu/dutchs/recmath/recmath.htm

**Prime Factoring**
www.delphiforfun.org/Programs/Factors.htm

**Factoring—Greatest Common Factor (GCF)—First Glance**
www.math.com/school/subject1/lessons/S1U3L2GL.html

**Greatest Common Factor**
www.aaamath.com/fra66g-grt-com-fac.html

**Greatest Common Factor (GCF)**
www.harcourtschool.com/glossary/ math/definitions/greatest.html

**Factoring—Least Common Multiple (LCM)—First Glance**
www.math.com/school/subject1/lessons/S1U3L3GL.html

**Least Common Multiple**
www.aaamath.com/g8-66i-lcm.html

**Lessons on Integers From Math Goodies**
www.mathgoodies.com/lessons/toc_vol5.shtm

**Integers**
www.mathleague.com/help/integers/integers.htm

**2.1 Integers**
www.dgp.toronto.edu/people/mooncake/thesis/node16.html

# CHAPTER 7

# MEASUREMENT

## DIFFERENCE BETWEEN ARBITRARY
## AND STANDARD UNITS

Measurement is the determination of the size of a thing counted in standard units, such as inches, pounds, or minutes, and it is one of the most practical applications of mathematics. Individuals can set up needed units of measurement, based on arbitrary units such as paper clips, for example, or on the length of a particular piece of string, the size of a particular cup or glass, or the height of particular animal. Students can measure how many erasers wide a desk is, how many sneakers long a work table is, or how many spelling books heavy a science book is. However, standard sizes are needed if a measure is to be useful to the whole society, rather than just to the individual.

## HISTORIC MEASUREMENT

Just as the skill of measurement and a system of standardized measurement are important to modern life and commerce, historically, they were vital to the development of trade and record keeping. Various societies have had many idiosyncratic ways of measuring.

Early Egyptians mastered measuring (or surveying), both for fields whose boundary marks had been flooded by the Nile, and for the building of the pyramids. The Egyptians used knotted ropes, the *merkhet* (somewhat like a yardstick, made of a split center rib of a palm leaf), and measuring rods to indicate length, which was measured in royal cubits (a cubit was the length of a forearm from wrist to elbow). A cubit equalled 7 palms (the width of a hand excluding the thumb), and one palm equalled 4 digits (a finger's breadth). These palms and finger breadths were similar to what later evolved in Greece. The Greeks also used the concept of a foot, which, depending upon the part of Greece, equalled between 27 and 35 centimeters.

Further east, in Mesopotamia, the Sumerians and Babylonians had a base 60 number system, and they also measured in cubits, based on digits (finger breadths), but did not use feet. Sixty digits made up a double cubit, while 60 double cubits made up a cord, the largest linear unit. Many building measurements were in units of 12 cubits, which equalled about 6 meters (or about 18 feet). These inhabitants of the Tigris-Euphrates River Valley were enthusiastic traders, so they also originated standard measurements of weight, volume, area, and length.

The Greeks, as mentioned, were concerned with measurement, and the word "geometry" translates as "measuring of the earth." Their lengths of measurement included the finger breadth, the palm, and the foot, as well as much larger measurements such as the *plethron* (100 linear feet or 10,000 square feet).

The Romans also used the idea of a finger's breadth, four of which equalled a palm, and the concept of a foot. Their foot was just over 33 centimeters, named the *pes Drusianus,* after a stepson of Augustus, but they also had the "short foot" of 29.42 centimeters. Because they were great road builders with a large empire, they chose to measure road distances by the army's marching, hence, 5 feet equalled a double *pace.* It was the Romans who conceived the idea of division by 12, and the Latin word for 12, *uncia,* meaning "unit," was the origin of the English words "ounce" (originally one-twelfth of a pound) and "inch" (still one-twelfth of a foot, and roughly the diameter of a thumb). The Roman calendar alternated between 10 and 12 months, and after many years of shifting, Julius Caesar finally settled on the current 12, including leap year. The Romans also set down the idea of the pound (our current abbreviation "lb" comes from the Latin *libra pondo* or "in weight").

By about 800 A.D., the Arabs were using Hindu numerals. In Western Europe measurement varied from country to country, and even within countries, throughout the Middle Ages and up through the Renaissance. France, for example, did not begin to standardize its measurements, weights, and even time zones, until the 1600s, and did not complete standardization until the 1800s, with the metric system first adopted by a revolutionary government in 1791.

## IMPERIAL AND U.S. MEASUREMENT

Although many English and European measurements came from the ancients, there was considerable variation. The English foot, for example, was longer than the standard Roman foot, what had been the

Roman double pace (5 feet) instead became the English yard of 3 feet, and the English mile became 5,280 feet (because the foot measurement was longer). The English and American measurement of the acre, standardized about 1305, is also derived from the Roman, but the surveyors' poles used to measure land length were different sizes for the Romans and the English, giving the English acre about 4,840 square yards or 43,560 square feet.

England held onto its unique "imperial" measurements (which increasingly differed from those in the United States) until quite recently, finally switching to the metric system in the 1970s. American measurement, with some differences (notably in money and in measuring volume), largely was adopted from the British system during the colonial period, with some ensuing changes. The American gallon, for example, based on the old English wine gallon of 231 cubic inches, is smaller than the English Imperial gallon. The current United States standard system of measurement was put into law by Congress in 1832.

## THE METRIC SYSTEM

As noted, the government of France early in the French Revolution was the first to adopt the metric system (based on ten) in 1791, although the basic measurements had been in place since the work of French scientists in the latter 1600s. The metric system was promoted by Napoleon in the early 1800s when he conquered most of Europe, which is why it did not spread to unconquered Great Britain or to the United States. But since Great Britain converted to the metric system in the 1970s, the United States is an oddity in that the metric system is in very minor use here. This makes trade with the rest of the world somewhat more difficult than it should be, since most former European colonies in Africa, Asia, and Latin America have also adopted the metric system. The post-World War II push to adopt the metric system in the United States long has been resisted. Those students who were told in the 1950s that they had to learn the metric system because its adoption was imminent are still waiting.

Current metric measurement differs somewhat from the earlier standard, in which the length of a meter was based on measurement of a length of one minute of the earth's arc, with the centimeter and kilometer based on multiples of the length of the meter (currently 1 meter is approximately 1.093 of a yard). The length and weight of the meter and the kilogram, in particular, have been redefined several times. Other commonly used elements of the metric system are the centimeter (approximately .3937 of an inch) and the kilometer (approximately .621 of a mile).

Metric measures are easy to handle, since they are based on powers of ten. All length measurements are pegged to the length of the meter, either larger (kilometer) or smaller (centimeters or millimeters), and in that relationship, they show the full power of the decimal system. The rough guide for those unfamiliar with the metric system is that a meter is a little longer than a yard, an inch is about 2 and a half centimeters, and a kilometer is roughly six-tenths of a mile. "Milli" is the prefix meaning "one-thousandth," "centi" is the prefix meaning "one-hundredth," and "deci" is the prefix meaning "one-tenth." Additionally, "kilo" is the prefix meaning "one thousand," "hecto" is the prefix for "one hundred," and "deka" is the prefix for "ten." These prefixes are true for meters (length), grams (weight), and liters (volume), and, once familiar, they make the metric system easy to use. There is no real need for students to memorize conversions or to practice the tasks of conversion between the U.S. system and the metric system, as long as they understand how each works and have an idea of rough approximates for the most common usages (such as liters or kilometers).

## PREPARING TO MEASURE

Since there are many different things that may need to be measured, it is first important to be clear on whether the student is measuring length (or height), weight, area, capacity (liquid or dry measure), time, or distance (another version of length). Before beginning, the student should know how to do basic mathematical operations, since adding, subtracting, multiplying, and dividing are needed to handle various measurements. The two major elements of measuring are choosing a unit, and then, through one or more operations, finding the number of units in the object to be measured. That number is the answer.

## Linear Measurement (Length and Height)

Length is perhaps the easiest element to measure, so it is usually the first one presented. Items of various lengths, both obvious and misleading, can be lined up and compared, and in this regard, estimating is a valuable skill that will lead the way to more careful measurement and calculation. American linear measurement is usually in inches, feet, or miles, although any standard unit can be used. Undesignated units are used in most of the examples in this chapter.

But what happens when items cannot be lined up to be compared? A measuring tool such as a ruler can be used to measure each item, then the measurements are compared. Once the students understand the concept of a ruler, they can move on to working with rulers that have been calibrated in either inches or centimeters. An architect's ruler is a lot of fun, because it is both long and three-dimensional (triangular), and usually has at least six different length calibrations.

A similar measurement to length is height, which is simply length turned in another direction, typically vertical rather than horizontal. Putting length and height in the same example would result in a drawing of a right angle, in this particular example with a length of 3 for one side and a height of 4 for the other.

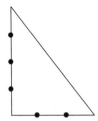

## Area Measurement

Area is usually measured in square inches, feet, or miles, so the only new fact likely to be needed in measuring area is that 43,560 square feet = 1 acre. If the drawing began above is completed with another right angle, it becomes a rectangle (a figure with four right angles, in which the two opposing sides are equal in length). This drawing would also work with a square, which has four equal sides, but there is no distinction between length and height in such a figure, so an oblong (a rectangle with two sides shorter than the other two) is a better choice with which to begin:

A student could multiply the length by the height (3 × 5) to get the number of units in the total area (15 square inches). This skill is very helpful in measuring square footage of rooms or walls for carpet or paint, and there are many other instances when being able to find the area of a rectangle's surface is useful. Students should have the opportunity to cut up the various figures and move them around, to learn that changing the shape does not affect the total area. This knowledge will be particularly valuable when dealing with more complex shapes such as triangles or circles.

Once a student has learned to measure the area of rectangle, the same right angle can be revisited:

By simply multiplying the height by the length, then dividing the product (the area of a full rectangle) by 2, the student can find the area of a triangle. If desired, another triangle can be drawn in on top of the first, to illustrate clearly that a triangle is, indeed, half of a rectangle, and that the two halves are being shown (a geoboard which is a square board with pegs arranged so that rubber bands can be stretched over them to outline shapes, is even more helpful in showing aspects of triangles than of rectangles):

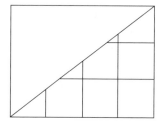

These calculations hold true for all triangles, but the right triangle illustrates them the best. On other triangles, two smaller triangles (which combined will equal the first triangle), instead of the one additional right triangle, may need to be drawn in on either side (or added to the geoboard) to form a complete rectangle:

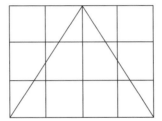

Finding the area of a circle is considerably more difficult, and is not usually presented until middle school. The formula A=pi $r^2$ (or A = $\Pi r^2$) indicates that the area equals approximately 3 (actually, 3.1416 carried to many more places) times the radius times itself (the radius is the distance from the center of the circle to any point on the outer edge). In the following example, the formula reads A = 3.1416 × $5^2$ or A = 3.1416 × 25 = 78.5400 units$^2$ or square units:

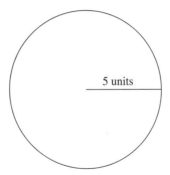

5 units

## Perimeter Measurement

To find the distance around a rectangle, known as the "perimeter," the student can measure all 4 sides, then add them (3 + 3 + 4 + 4) to get the total number of units (14, in this case, typically presented in inches or centimeters) in the perimeter.

Since a rectangle has two equal lengths and two equal heights, a student also could multiply two times the length (4 × 2) and two times the height (3 × 2), then add the sums (8 + 6) to get the total number of units in the perimeter (14). Or, if each of the four sides were the same length, the length of one side could simply be multiplied by four. Hence, the saying that "Every rectangle is a multiplication problem," referring to area.

The perimeters of a triangle and of a circle are rather more sophisticated. The perimeter is still the sum of the sides on any triangle, but on a right triangle, although the two short sides (a and b) are easy to measure, the longest side (c), the "hypotenuse," is often not a whole number, so it is difficult for beginners to measure. An easier formula for right triangles is that the square of each of the shorter sides added together equals the square of the hypotenuse of the longest side ($a^2 + b^2 = c^2$).

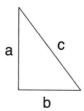

Finding the perimeter, known as the "circumference," of a circle is not ordinarily taught to children in the elementary grades, since it, too, is somewhat complex. The formula "$C = \Pi\, d$" indicates that the circumference equals $\Pi$ (3.1416) times the diameter, as in the example below:

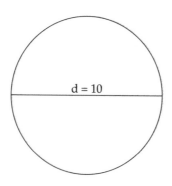

d = 10

## Volume Measurement

Volume is the space taken up by a three-dimensional form (such as a block), and interior volume is the space contained in such a form. There are many practical reasons for measuring volume in everyday life: content of packages, drinks (such as liters of soft drinks), gasoline, and recipes all deal with volume. Traditional building blocks, or even sugar cubes, are good for comparisons of volume in differently shaped structures, as are empty boxes that can be filled with smaller blocks for concrete examples of volume (finding the volume of round objects is much more complex). The mathematical process for finding volume is similar to that for finding area (length × height), with the addition of another dimension of measurement (width) to get the product (length × height × width). In the example below, the volume is $5 \times 3 \times 2 = 30$ cubic units.

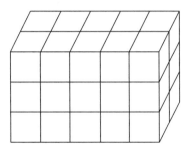

## Weight and Mass Measurement

Weight is an amount or quantity of heaviness or mass. Mass is the measure of the amount of matter in an object, while weight is the force of gravity acting on an object. It is important to note that mass is different from weight, and a good way to show that difference is to imagine that an item on the earth travels to the moon. The item still has the same mass, or amount of matter, but it will have a different weight on the moon because the force of gravity there is different since the moon is smaller than the earth. The metric system measures mass, not weight, and the kilogram is the standard unit for measuring mass, although the smaller gram unit also is very useful. A balance scale can be used to measure mass, first with vastly differing items, then with ones closer in weight.

The basic U.S. units for measuring weight are pounds and ounces. Weight is easy to judge if items of various weights, both obvious and misleading, can be held and compared. In this regard, as with judging length, estimating is a valuable skill that will lead the way to more careful measurement and calculation. Objects of decidedly different weights, objects that look the same but weigh different amounts, light objects that look heavy, or heavy objects that look light all can be used to examine the concept of weight. When the items are close in weight, the spring scale can be used.

## Time Measurement: Calendars

Another form of measurement is measuring days—365 of which make up a year. The year is marked off on a calendar, divided into 12 months, with 28 to 31 days in each month. Each month, in turn, has a little over 4 weeks, with each week made up of 7 days, and 52 weeks in the year. It is important to note that there is nothing immutable about the calendar measurements—different peoples in different cultures have measured long stretches of time differently. However, the units of 12 months based on the phases of the moon and fitted into the astronomical year were common in the ancient world and are now the standard almost everywhere.

Early Egyptians measured the year in 12 thirty-day months, with an addition of 5 days each year to keep their calendar in sync with astronomical observations (a year is 365 and one-quarter days, so every four years, the calendar is thrown off a day, unless some provision is made to account for the fractional day). The Babylonians were skilled astronomers who predicted eclipses and first recorded Halley's comet, and their calendar was made up of 12 lunar months (based on the cycles of the moon), with an extra month added occasionally. The Greeks also followed lunar months of 29 or 30 days, also with an extra month inserted when the calendar got too off-kilter, and their methods are still used in the West to figure the yearly date of Easter. The Romans, as noted above, refined the 12-month calendar under Julius Caesar, and named the months still used in the West.

The Julian calendar was used throughout Europe until it was realigned by Pope Gregory XIII in 1582. Pope Gregory XIII came up with a plan to keep the calendar accurate in the future by the institution of Leap Year—adding a day to the month of February every 4 years to account for the fractions in the orbit of the earth. This so-called Gregorian calendar was adopted all over Europe, although the English and their American colonies did not adopt it until 1752.

## Time Measurement: Telling Time

The ancients used a variety of methods to tell time: sundials (which measured the direction of a shadow cast by the sun), water clocks (which measured how long it took water to drip out of a bowl), and hour glasses (which measured how long it took sand to run out of a specially shaped glass). The Babylonians divided their days into 12 equal parts (which the Romans called "horo," or hour), divided the hours into 60 smaller parts (which the Romans called "minuta," or minutes), and divided those into 60 still smaller parts (which the Romans called "secunda," or seconds), but there was no very accurate way to measure any of these.

By the Middle Ages, however, weight-driven clocks were common in churches, and eventually more accurate pendulum clocks became standard. The traditional clock is one interesting and practical use of the circumference of a circle, in which the circumference is divided into 60 minutes (based on the ancient base 60 system). "Pocket clocks," or watches, were invented in Germany during the Renaissance by Peter Henlein in 1511, who invented the clock spring. The pocket watches were expensive, popular pieces of jewelry for those who could afford them. During World War I, strapping the watch on the wrist was found to be more efficient, and in the 1920s, wristwatches became the norm throughout the western world. In the late 1940s, the inexpensive quartz clock was invented and became the most common type of time measurement for watches, computers, and other electronic equipment.

Time is an abstract concept, and for that reason learning to tell time can be difficult for the uninitiated. For most children, practice in sequencing events and understanding duration of time are important skills to be learned before formally learning to tell time on a dial clock (digital clocks make it easy to tell the time, but do not ensure understanding of the concept). Memory is a factor in sequencing, so asking a student to describe steps in making something simple or to describe in order a course of events he or she took part in recently can help develop memory and sequencing skills.

Another exercise is to have the child estimate which of two activities will take longer: combing one's hair or eating lunch? One activity helpful to understanding chronology is the personal timeline: when was the child born, the dog acquired, the apartment moved into, the baby born? By sequencing these events, the child gains an understanding of the passage of time.

## Temperature Measurement

Temperature is another often-used item of measurement. Temperature is usually measured in degrees, using Gabriel Daniel Fahrenheit's mercury-in-a-glass thermometer system, invented in Germany in 1714. The United States uses the Fahrenheit system, in which water's freezing point is designated as 32 degrees (the coldest temperature achievable using a mixture of ice and salt), and its boiling point as 212 degrees, with a normal human blood temperature designated 98.6 (originally and erroneously 96 degrees). This system is popular for measurement because of its small, therefore accurate, increments, with 180 degrees between freezing and boiling.

The Reaumur scale, invented by the Frenchman R. A. F. Reamur, is much less widely used, as it only has 80 degrees between freezing and boiling. However, the centigrade scale invented by the Swedish astronomer Anders Celsius is the standard in most of the world. The centigrade thermometer designates water's freezing point as zero degrees, and its boiling point as 100 degrees.

## Money Measurement/Counting

The concept of money is thought to have originated in the Mesopotamian part of the Middle East with the Lydians in the seventh century B.C. Certainly, King Croesus was circulating money there by the mid-fifth century B.C. In many parts of the world, in both ancient and modern times, value might be measured by any number of measures, including trinkets, horses, women, or number of sheep or cattle.

But even in ancient times, it soon became apparent that trading one needed item for another ("bartering") quickly became unwieldy, involving too many trades and too much time to find compatible people and products. Most societies developed the idea of money with a particular value (a form of measurement), which could be swapped for any item, greatly simplifying trade. Usually, some sort of metal or standard weight was used as money, but any item would do, as along as there was agreement as to its worth.

Almost every country in the world has its own monetary system, although often a country's money's value is pegged to that of a larger neighbor. Clearly, it is very much to a country's advantage to have a stable and accepted system of money, so other countries will be willing to trade with it. The United States is very influential, partly because it is one of the largest trading nations in the world.

Interestingly, although the United States is not on the metric system, its monetary system is very simple and easy to understand, as it is decimal based—the smallest unit is the penny, and the largest unit is the dollar. Within those parameters, 100 pennies equal 1 dollar, and dollars can be counted in ones, tens, hundreds, thousands, millions, billions, and trillions. Besides the 100 pennies used to make up a dollar, there are coins in the amount of 5 cents, 10 cents, 25 cents, and 50 cents. Dollar bills in common circulation are limited to ones, fives, tens, twenties, fifties, and hundreds, although larger bills are used within banks.

**CURRENT STANDARD AMERICAN MEASUREMENTS:**
*Length and Distance:*
1 inch is the smallest common measurement
12 inches = 1 foot
3 feet = 1 yard
5 and a half yards (16 and a half feet)= 1 rod
40 rods = 1 furlong (note: rods and furlongs are not commonly used)
8 furlongs = 5,280 feet (1760 yards) = 1 mile

*Weight:*
1 ounce is the smallest common measurement
16 ounces = 1 pound
2000 pounds = 1 short ton (although in sea shipping, 1 ton = 40 cubic feet)
2240 pounds = 1 long ton

Volume can be confusing, as ounces, for example, are used for weight as well as volume, so an ounce can be 1/16 of a pound or 1/16 of a pint.

*Volume: Fluid measures*
1 cup = 8 fluid ounces
2 cups = 1 pint (16 fluid ounces)
2 pints = 1 quart (or 4 cups or 32 fluid ounces)
2 quarts = one half gallon (2 quarts or 64 fluid ounces)
4 quarts = one gallon (or 4 quarts or 128 fluid ounces—gallons are used only for liquid measurement)

*Volume: Dry measures*
1 cup = 8 dry ounces
2 cups = 1 dry pint

1 dry quart = 2 dry pints
8 dry quarts = 1 peck (16 dry pints)
2 pecks = one-half bushel (8 dry quarts)
1 bushel = 4 pecks (pecks and bushels are used only for dry measurement)

**COMMON METRIC MEASUREMENTS:**
*Linear:*
10 millimeters = 1 centimeter
10 centimeters = 1 decimeter
10 decimeters = 1 meter
10 meters = 1 dekameter
10 dekameters = 1 hectometer = 100 meters
10 hectometers = 1 kilometer = 1,000 meters

*Area:*
100 square millimeters = 1 square centimeter
10,000 square centimeters = 1 square meter
100 square meters = 1 are
100 ares = 1 hectare = 10,000 square meters
100 hectares = 1 square kilometer = 1,000,000 square meters

*Volume:*
10 milliliters = 1 centiliter
10 centiliters = 1 deciliter = 100 milliliters
10 deciliters = 1 liter = 1, 000 milliliters

*Mass:*
10 milligrams = 1 centigram
10 centigrams = 1 decigram = 100 milligrams
10 decigrams = 1 gram = 1,000 milligrams
10 grams = 1 dekagram
10 dekagrams = 1 hectogram = 100 grams
10 hectograms = 1 kilogram = 1000 grams
1,000 kilograms = 1 metric ton

**COMMON APPROXIMATIONS OF AMERICAN STANDARD WITH METRIC:**

| | |
|---|---|
| 1 yard to 0.9114 meters | 1 meter to 1.0936 yards |
| 1 lb. to 0.4535 kilograms | 1 kilogram to 2.2046 lbs. |
| 1 gallon to 3.785 liters | 1 liter to 0.2641 gallons |
| 1 bushel to 35.238 liters | 1 liter to 0.0283 bushels |
| 1 mile to 1.609 kilometers | 1 kilometer to 0.621 miles |

## READING FOR STUDENTS

Adams, P. (1989). *Ten Beads Tall.* Sudbury, MA: Child's Play International.

Adler, D. A. (1975). *Three-d, Two-d, One-d.* New York: Thomas Y. Crowell Publishers.

Allington, R. L. and Connor, E. (1979). *Opposites.* Milwaukee, WI: Raintree Publications.

Allington, R. L., Krull, K., and Spangler, N. (1983). *Measuring.* Milwaukee, WI: Raintree Publications.

Ardley, N. (1983). *Making Metric Measurements.* New York: Franklin Watts.

Anno, Mitsumasa. (1995). *Anno's Magic Seeds.* New York: Philomel Books.

Arnold, C. and Johnson, P. (1984). *Measurements: Fun, Facts, and Activities.* New York: Franklin Watts.

Axelrod, A. and McGinley-Nally, S. (1999). *Pigs in the Pantry: Fun with Math and Cooking.* Glenview, IL: Scott Foresman.

Axelrod, A. (1998). *Pigs on a Blanket: Fun with Math and Time.* New York: Aladdin Books.

Axelrod, A. (1997). *Pigs will be Pigs: Fun with Math and Money.* Glenview, IL: Scott Foresman.

Birch, David. (1998). *The King's Pressboard.* New York: Puffin.

Branley, F. M. and Lustig, L. (1975). *Measure with Metric.* New York: Thomas Y. Crowell Publishers.

Branley, F. M. and Barton, B. (1976). *How Little and How Much: A Book about Scales.* New York: Thomas Y. Crowell Publishers.

Cantienti, B. and Gachter, F. (1981). *Little Elephant and Big Mouse.* Saxonville, MA: Picture Book Studio.

Clement, R. (1991). *Counting on Frank.* Milwaukee, WI: Gareth Stevens Publishing.

Fey, J. and Russel, J. (1971). *Long, Short, High, Low, Thin, Wide.* New York: Thomas Y. Crowell Publishers.

Froman, R. and Barton, B. (1976). *Angles are Easy as Pie.* New York: Thomas Y. Crowell Publishers.

Greenfield, E. and Gilchrist, J. S. (1991). *Big Friend, Little Friend.* New York: Black Butterfly Children's Books.

Hoban, T. (1972). *Push, Pull, Empty, Full: A Book of Opposites.* New York: Macmillan Publishing Co.

Hoban, T. (1985). *Is it Larger? Is it Smaller?* New York: Greenwillow Books.

Hoban, T. (1990). *Exactly the Opposite.* New York: Greenwillow Books.

Laithwaite, E. (1988). *Size: The Measure of Things.* New York: Franklin Watts.

Lamm, J. (1974). *Let's Talk about the Metric System.* Middle Village, NY: Jonathan David Publishers.

Leaf, M. (1976). *Metric Can be Fun.* Philadelphia, PA: J. B. Lippincott Co.

Linn, C. F. and Madden, D. (1972). *Estimation.* New York: Thomas Y. Crowell Publications.

Manley, D. and Astrop, J. (1979). *The Other Side.* Milwaukee, WI: Raintree Publications.

Moncure, J. B. and Friedman, J. (1988). *The Biggest Snowball of All.* Chicago: Children's Press.

Matthews, Rupert. (2000). *Telling the Time.* New York: Franklin Watts.

Myllar, R. (1991). *How Big is a Foot?* New York: Dell Publishing.

Neuschwander, C. and Geehan, W. (2001). *Sir Cumference and the Great Knight of Angleland.* Watertown, MA: Charlesbridge Publishing.

Petty, K. and Kopper, L. (1987). *What's that Size?* New York: Franklin Watts.

Piankowski, J. (1990). *Sizes.* New York: Little Simon.

Pluckrose, H. and Fairclough, C. (1987). *Big and Little*. New York: Franklin Watts.

Pluckrose, H. and Fairclough, C. (1988). *Capacity*. New York: Franklin Watts.

Pluckrose, H. and Fairclough, C. (1988). *Length*. New York: Franklin Watts.

Scarry, R. (1976). *Short and Tall*. Racine, WI: Western Publishing Co.

Schneider, H., Schneider N., and Shimin, S. (1946). *How Big is Big?* Reading, MA: Addison-Wesley Publishing Co.

Schwartz, D. M. and Kellogg, S. (1985). *How Much is a Million?* New York: Lothrop, Lee & Shepherd Books.

Schwartz, D. M. and Kellogg, S. (1989). *If You Made a Million*. New York: Lothrop, Lee & Shepherd Books.

Shapp, M., Shapp, C., and Nicklaus, C. (1975). *Let's Find Out about What's Big and What's Small*. New York: Franklin Watts.

Shapp, M. & Shapp, C. (1975). *Let's Find Out about What's Light and What's Heavy*. New York: Franklin Watts.

Shimek, W. J. and Overlie, G. (1975). *The Liter*. Minneapolis, MN: Lerner Publications Co.

Spier, P. (1972). *Fast-slow, High-low: A Book of Opposites*. New York: Doubleday & Co.

Schmandt-Besserat, D. (1999). *The History of Counting*. New York: Morrow Junior Books.

Schwartz, D. (1998). *G is for Googol: A Math Alphabet Book*. Berkeley, CA: Tricycle Press.

Skurzynski, G. (2000). *On Time: From Seasons to Split Seconds*. Washington, D.C.: National Geographic Society.

Srivastava, J. J. and Lustig, L. (1980). *Spaces, Shapes, and Sizes*. New York: Thomas Y. Crowell Publishers.

Szieszka, J. and Smith, L. (1995). *Math Curse*. New York: Penguin Books.

Youldon, G. (1982). *Sizes*. New York: Franklin Watts.

---

## WEBSITES

**Measurement**
www.theteacherscorner.net/math/measurement/index.htm

**Money**
www.theteacherscorner.net/math/money/index.htm

**Measurement**
www.aaamath.com/B/mea.htm

**Money**
www.aaamath.com/B/mny.htm

**Measurements converter**
www.convert-me.com/en/

**Graphing**
www.theteacherscorner.net/math/graphing/index.htm

**Temperature, Graphing**
www.buildingrainbows.com/CA/lesson/lessonid/1013100847

**Graphs**
www.aaamath.com/B/gra.htm

**Time**
www.theteacherscorner.net/math/time/index.htm

**Teacher Workshops**
www.miamisci.org/rise/kineticsculptures.html

**Teachers Guide—November**
emma.la.asu.edu/EDUCATION/rpconline/rpc/november96/nov96te.pdf

**Frame Work**
www.motion-vision.com/dvt1/framework.htm

# CHAPTER 8

# GEOMETRY AND SPATIAL SENSE

Geometry is the study of the properties and relationships that exist with two-dimensional or three-dimensional objects. Learning about geometry typically begins at a young age and develops into a formal investigation of the subject as the years pass. Unfortunately, some teachers spend limited time on the study of geometry in favor of devoting that time to practice with algorithms and whole number operations. This practice has changed in recent years; however, it remains true that most adults do not have a fully developed understanding of geometry.

## INFORMAL GEOMETRY

The term "informal geometry" is used to describe a wide range of geometric activities that take place at the elementary and middle grade levels. These activities give students opportunities to build, explore, take apart, and investigate shapes in the world around them. Although the activities may be approached with varying degrees of sophistication, they are designed with investigation, exploration, and hands-on activities at their core.

### Spatial Sense

Spatial sense is one aspect of geometry that deals with intuition about shapes and the relationships among shapes. Through informal geometric activities, spatial sense is developed by investigating the characteristics of shapes and how they act in the environment.

The concepts of geometry usually deal within two broad spectrums—solid geometry and plane geometry.

## Solid Geometry

Solid geometry is the study of solids, or three-dimensional shapes. Toys, blocks, balls, and other objects are the first solid models that most children encounter.

## Describing and Classifying Objects

The beginning activities of solid geometry center on the characteristics of solid models. Blocks are examples of rectangular prisms. An examination and description of their features yields sides or faces that are smooth, with opposite faces congruent in size. Two faces intersect on an edge that is not smooth. Three edges intersect at a point. Describing the characteristics of solids provides the opportunity for the introduction of vocabulary, terminology that is given meaning because of the concrete example available.

Many three-dimensional objects are present in the world around us. As noted, blocks and boxes are rectangular prisms, or special types of rectangular prisms called cubes. Balls are spheres. Ice cream comes in cones. A tube from inside a roll of paper towels is a cylinder.

Once the characteristics of a model are recognized, the student can compare the characteristics of more than one model. This process provides the beginning of classification. "They all have six faces," is a observable characteristic of multiple models. By recognizing similar and different features, the student can classify models by their geometric names, and can develop a better understanding of three-dimensional objects.

## Constructing Objects

Once a student is able to recognize characteristics of three-dimensional objects, a further complex step is the ability to construct them. The process of putting paper, toothpicks, and other objects together to make three-dimensional figures requires a great depth of thinking and understanding. Using a two-dimensional pattern, and cutting and folding to create three-dimensional figures is yet another important step that requires not only a thorough understanding of solid shapes, but the ability to think about the solid shapes in abstract situations. The two-dimensional patterns used to make three-dimensional solids are called networks.

## Relating Three Dimensions to Two Dimensions

A final aspect of solid geometry, that is used by architects, city planners, and designers, to name a few, is being able to visualize a portion of a three-dimensional solid as a two-dimensional shape. This is the ability to identify a solid, given the shape of a side, as well as the ability to visualize a cross section. These skills rely on strong familiarity with shapes and abstractions.

## Plane Geometry

Plane geometry is the type of geometry most commonly taught in schools. It is the geometry of flat surfaces, known as "planes." All figures in plane geometry are two-dimensional and can be drawn on a piece of paper.

## Properties of Shapes

The ability to recognize the properties of plane shapes is just as important as the ability to recognize shapes in solid geometry. Thorough familiarity with shapes, their characteristics, and their distinguishing attributes, helps develop a rich understanding of plane geometry.

## Number of Sides

Any closed figure that is a shape made up of straight sides, is called a "polygon." Polygons are classified by their number of sides, as in the table below:

| NUMBER OF SIDES | POLYGON |
|:---:|:---|
| 3 | Triangle |
| 4 | Quadrilateral |
| 5 | Pentagon |
| 6 | Hexagon |
| 8 | Octagon |
| 10 | Decagon |

## Number of Corners

As sides are investigated, it is easy to discover that in two-dimensional polygons, the sides meet each other at a corner or point. Taking this one step further, the number of corners is the same as the number of sides.

## Symmetry

There are two types of symmetry. The first type is "line symmetry". If a line passes through a shape, and the shape is the same on both sides of the line, it has line or "reflectional" symmetry. Two examples of line or reflectional symmetry are shown below (similarly, a butterfly is often used as an example to describe reflectional symmetry).

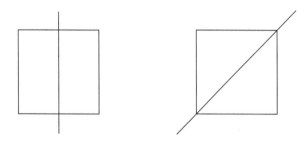

The other type of symmetry is "rotational symmetry." If a object can be turned, or rotated, around a point, and the object lands on top of itself, it has rotational symmetry. The point of rotation is important. A circle has rotational symmetry around the midpoint. However, it does not have rotational symmetry around any other point.

## Length of Sides

Often, the lengths of the sides are taken into consideration when shapes are being classified. For example, both a parallelogram (a quadrilateral having both pairs of opposite sides parallel to each other) and a rectangle (a parallelogram with four right angles) have opposite sides the same length, while a square has four sides the same length. Not only is measurement important to determine length, but so is comparison of the sides to determine congruence.

## Size of Angles

Angles of different sizes determine types of triangles, as well as characteristics of other polygons. An angle whose measurement is less than 90 degrees is an "acute angle." An angle equal to 90 degrees is a "right angle." All of the angles of squares and rectangles equal 90 degrees. An "obtuse angle" is an angle greater than 90 degrees. A triangle that has an obtuse angle is called an "obtuse triangle." Questions also may be used to think about the size of angles and the ways angles relate to shapes. Rather than memorizing facts about angles, the size of the angles may be thought of in relationship to the shapes of which they are a part. A question such as "Can you make a four-sided figure that does not have two angles greater than 40 degrees?" gives the student the opportunity to think about a shape as related to the angles that are part of it. With the question above, the student can make a four-sided figure that does not have two angles greater than 40 degrees. It would look like this:

### Parallel and Perpendicular

Other characteristics of plane shapes are parallel and perpendicular sides. Since these are characteristic of the sides of plane shapes, parallel and perpendicular sides are also characteristic of lines, segments, and rays.

Sides are parallel if they are equidistant, or the same distance, at all points on the line. Another way of thinking about this is that the lines will never touch. Sides are perpendicular if they intersect to form a right angle.

### Convexity and Concavity

Any polygon may be classified as "convex" or "concave." A polygon is convex if all of the interior angles are less than 180 degrees. A polygon is concave if one of the interior angles is greater than 180 degrees. In this latter case, the shape "caves in" on itself, as shown in the previous diagram.

### Altitude

Altitude is another name for height. The height depends on the side of the shape that is identified as the base. An altitude may be a side of the shape, or the length of a segment perpendicular to the identified base through the vertex opposite that base. For example, in a square or a right triangle that contains a 90 degree angle, the altitude is one of the sides. In the rectangle and the right triangle below, if the bottom sides are bases, then the vertical sides are altitudes. However, in the triangle, if the base is the sloping side opposite the right angle, as shown below, the altitude must be perpendicular to that side, so it may NOT be one of the other sides of the triangle. Rather, it must be a segment perpendicular to that side and through the opposite vertex, as shown:

## Naming Geometric Shapes

Understanding the characteristics of shapes is important. It is probably as important as remembering the names of the various shapes. Memorizing the names of the shapes can be a daunting task. Connecting the characteristics of various shapes with their names aids in memorization and understanding. For example, all closed figures with three sides are triangles.

## Relationships between Shapes: Congruent and Similar

When shapes with the same characteristics, for example, two triangles or two rectangles, are compared to one another, they may have no relationship with each other, or they may be either "congruent" or "similar."

Shapes that are congruent have the same size and shape. Their angles and their sides have the same measurements. If the shapes were placed on top of each other, the bottom shape would be covered completely, with no gaps and no overlaps.

Shapes are similar if their sides are in proportion to one another and their angles are equal and corresponding. Two shapes that appear to be alike may not be similar if they do not meet these criteria. This concept of similarity should not be studied until students have an understanding of ratio.

## Classifying Shapes

Using the characteristics of shapes and grouping them by their similarities is a process known as "classification." Three-sided shapes are triangles, four-sided shapes are quadrilaterals, and so on. The most common ways to characterize shapes are by sides and angles.

Classification of quadrilaterals is common. There are many different types of quadrilaterals and not all of the types are disjoint (meaning that they do not intersect and that there will be overlap); rather, many share characteristics. If a person is given a number of quadrilaterals and asked to classify them as squares and rectangles, some of the quadrilaterals will appear under both classifications. Given the characteristics that define the shapes, for example, the squares will be in the group of rectangles, but the rectangles will not be in the group of squares, as explained below.

Rectangles, squares, rhombuses, trapezoids, parallelograms, and kites are the most common types of quadrilaterals. When a rectangle is defined as a quadrilateral with opposite sides congruent and parallel and four right angles, that is a definition that also describes a square. However, if a square is defined as a quadrilateral with four congruent sides and four right angles, a rectangle cannot be a square. If a rectangle is defined as having ONLY two congruent sides then a square can not be a rectangle. It is easy to understand how confusion can arise. Once again, a focus on characteristics of the figures facilitates understanding.

---

### READINGS FOR STUDENTS

Burns, M. and Silveria, G. (1995). *The Greedy Triangle.* Glenview, IL: Pearson Learning.

Greenes, C., Dacey, L. S., & Spungin, R. (1999). *Spatial Sense (Hot Math Topics: Problem Solving, Communication, and Reasoning).* Palo Alto, CA: Dale Seymour Publishing.

Hill, E. (1986). *Spot Looks at Opposites.* New York: Putnam Publishing Group.

Hoban, T. (1991). *All about Where.* New York: Greenwillow Books.

Hoban, T. (1973). *Over, Under, and Through and Other Spatial Concepts.* New York: Macmillan Publishing Co.

Isaacson, P. M. (1988). *Round Buildings, Square Buildings, and Buildings That Wiggle Like a Fish.* New York: Knopf.

McMillan, B. (1986). *Becca Backward Frontward.* New York: Lothrop, Lee & Shepard Books.

Rogers, P. (1989). *The Shapes Game.* New York: Henry Holt.

Tester, S. R. and Fudala, R. M. (1977). *Over, Under, and All Around.* Elgin, IL: Child's World.

## WEBSITES

**Geometry**
www.theteacherscorner.net/math/geometry/index.htm

**Geometry**
www.aaamath.com/B/geo.htm

**Spacial Problems**
www.figurethis.org/

**Geometry and Spatial Sense**
www.linktolearning.com/geometry.htm

**1989 NCTM Standards: Grades K–4 Standard 9: Geometry and Spatial...**
standards.nctm.org/Previous/CurrEvStds/k4s9.htm

**Geometry & Spatial Sense**
garnet.acns.fsu.edu/~jflake/math/GeomSp/GeomSp.html

**Geometry—About Shape**
www.learner.org/teacherslab/math/geometry/shape/

**Geometry and Spatial Sense**
mathmetadata.org/ammtf/taxonomies/level1-draft.doc

**Mathematics: Geometry and Spatial Sense**
intech2000.miamisci.org/sss/ma/c24.php3

**Geometry and Spatial Sense**
www.mathteacherstore.com/middle/midlsoft/5-8math/titles/mtgs/
mtgsmain.htm

**Seven Numeracy Themes: Geometry: Spatial Sense and Measurement**
www.std.com/anpn/frame7.html

**Grade One Central (Geometry and Spatial Sense)**
www.geocities.com/GradeOne_ca/Lessons/geo.html

**Geometry and Spatial Sense (Strand C)**
fcit.coedu.usf.edu/FCAT5M/TeachRes/bibs/geometry.htm

**NCTM 2000—Standard 3—Geometry & Spatial Sense**
teams.lacoe.edu/standards2/standards/national/nat_std3_geo_k-2.html

**Geometry and Spatial Sense**
www.cctt.org/algebralessons/standard3.htm

**Geometry & Spatial Sense**
www.edu.gov.on.ca/eng/document/curricul/curr97ma/geometry.html

**Shape and Space in Geometry**
www.learner.org/teacherslab/math/geometry/across.html

**AIMS Math Connections: Series A**
www.aimsedu.org/workshops/week/seriesA.html

**Teachers of Mathematics Standards Addressed by PASCO Bundles**
www.pasco.com/standards/teach_res/standards/national/stds_mid_Math.
html

**PBS TeacherSource—Mathline**
www.pbs.org/teachersource/mathline/tips/tips0500.shtm

**Mathematics—Number Sense, Measurement and Spatial Sense**
www.memphis-schools.k12.tn.us/admin/tlapages/math_topic.htm

**Everyday Mathematics: Content by Strands**
www.sra-4kids.com/everydaylearning/em/infofor/strands/

**Geometry and Spatial Sense**
www.gecdsb.on.ca/d&g/math/Math%20Menus/gr1gass.htm

**Mathematics, Geometry and Spatial Sense**
www.state.nj.us/njded/frameworks/math/math5.pdf

**Go Fly a Kite Teacher's Page**
www.planemath.com/activities/flykite/kiteteachers.html

# CHAPTER 9

# DATA ANALYSIS AND PROBABILITY

Data is information that can be used to solve problems as well as analyze situations. Data analysis includes the comparisons between, representations of, and conclusions made regarding data, usually in the form of graphing, but also in the form of statistical tests. The ability to properly "do something" with the data is important, but no less important is the ability to understand what others have done with data. Newspapers and magazines contain tables, charts, and graphs that present information. Mathematical literacy includes having familiarity with various informational formats, in addition to possessing the ability to understand both the stories the information is intended to tell and the validity of the message.

## GRAPHING

There are many types of graphs, and often they cannot be used interchangeably with one another, since each is designed to convey specific information to a reader. An understanding of graphing includes the ability to construct, read, and interpret many types of graphs.

All graphs, no matter the type, contain a title that tells a reader what the graph is about. Most graphs also have a scale that indicates relative sizes and relationships. Scales vary depending on the type of graph.

### Pictographs/Picture Graphs

Picture graphs use pictures to represent information. The scale in a picture graph tells the value of each picture in the graph. Occasionally, the pictures represent one item or unit, but, more commonly, each of the pictures is worth more than one, so the scale must be taken into consideration in interpreting the graph. A pictograph represents discrete data. Pictographs are often used because of their visual appeal or impact. The same data that is represented in a pictograph can also be represented in a bar graph. Following is an example of a picture graph that shows the favorite fruit of each student in a kindergarten class.

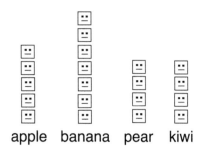

apple   banana   pear   kiwi

## Bar Graphs

A bar graph also represents discrete (made up of distinct or specific numbers) data: the information is countable. Bar graphs are easy to make and easy to understand. An example of a bar graph is below:

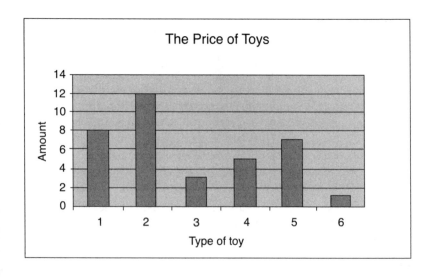

A histogram is a bar graph that shows frequency data along consecutive intervals. The following histogram is the graph of temperatures recorded at hourly intervals for a 12 hour time span, with temperature being the independent variable, or the value recorded on the horizontal x-axis. In this example, the temperature readings were 51, 54, 52, 56, 60, 61, 61, 62, 60, 60, and 59. Since temperature is shown along the x-axis, the temperatures from 51 to 62 are separated into equal intervals along that axis. The vertical y-axis indicates the frequency with which the temperatures in a given range occurred.

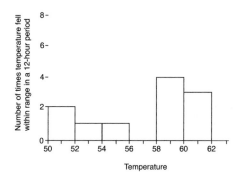

## Line Graphs

A line graph represents trends in data. Points are plotted to represent two related pieces of data and a line is drawn to connect the points.

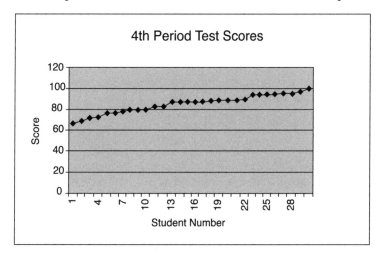

## Circle Graphs

Circle graphs represent data that has been partitioned into a part of the whole. Circle graphs are also called "pie graphs," since the divisions are typically shaped like pie slices. The total data is considered as 100 percent, then each of the quantities is a percentage of that total. An example of a circle graph is below:

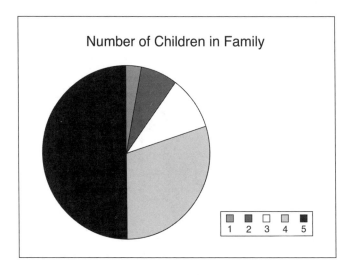

## Stem and Leaf Plots

Stem and leaf plots are a special type of bar graph. In the example of a stem and leaf plot below, the data is plotted by using the actual data to form a graph. In the example below, the numbers in the tens (far left) column form the stem (2, 3, 5, 6), and the 14 data values in the ones place (21, 22, 22, 24, 25, 33, 34, 35, 51, 51, 51, 52, 52, 60) become the leaves.

|   |         |
|---|---------|
| 2 | 1 2 2 4 5 |
| 3 | 3 4 5 |
| 5 | 1 1 1 2 2 |
| 6 | 0 |

Just as on a tree, the stems have multiple leaves (the 14 data values in the ones place). Stem and leaf plots can be an efficient way to represent data. In addition, they can be easy to interpret because none of the data is lost.

## Box and Whisker Plots

An easy method of visually displaying data that shows the median, range, and variance of the data is called a "box and whisker plot." The box contains the middle half of the data, one-fourth to the left and one-fourth to the right of the median that appears inside the box as a line. A line extends from the lower end of the box to the lowest extreme of the data and a line extends from the upper end of the box to the highest extreme of the data. Box and whisker plots are really pictures of statistics rather than pictures of data. An example of a box and whisker plot that represents the ages in months of a group of sixth grade students appears below, in which the lowest bound is 130, the highest bound is 154, and the median is 142 months.

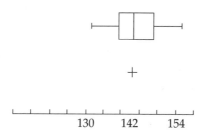

## PROBABILITY

Probability is the study of chance. Ideas about chances begin long before formal study of probability begins in school.

## Vocabulary

Early comprehension of probability develops through an understanding of vocabulary. Terms like "likely," "unlikely," "possible," "impossible," "certain," and "uncertain" all describe the potential for events to occur. "It is likely to rain," or "It is impossible that the sea is purple," are mathematical descriptions of the chance that events will occur.

## Randomness

Events are "random" if each of the items in a data set has the same chance of occurring. Rolling a die is a random event because each side of the die has the same chance of landing face up.

## Event

An "event" is an occurrence. Tossing a coin is an event. Rolling a die is an event.

## Independence of Events

Events may either be independent of or dependent on one another. An example of independent events is tossing a coin two times. What happens the second time the coin is tossed is not affected by the results of the first coin toss. Therefore, the second event is independent of the first event.

  If one event is dependent on another event, the outcome of the second event is affected by what happens in the first event. An example of a dependent event would be a situation that if given five balls in a container, one red, one white, one blue, one green, and one yellow, and single balls are picked multiple times without replacement, the second and consecutive events are dependent on what happens during the first or previous occurrences. For example, if a white ball is chosen the first pick, and not replaced, there are not as many balls or the same types of balls available for the second pick. Thus, the outcome of the second pick is a dependent event. Its outcome depends on the results of the first event.

## Statistics

Numbers that describe data are called statistics. They are measures of the data that quantify an attribute of the data set.

## Measures of Central Tendency

Measures of central tendency are used to describe groups of data. They are often called averages. The mean, median, and mode are various forms of averages dealt with below. How a person wishes to think about averages determines which of the methods is used to find an average.

## Mean

A "mean" is the most common average that is used, and a form of average that can be found in books, media, and classrooms. The mean is the number that represents what all of the data would look like if it were to be leveled out or equally distributed. It is also described by the procedure used to calculate it. It is the sum of a set of numbers divided by the quantity of numbers. For example, the mean of the numbers 3, 5, 9, 8, 2, 3 is 30/6 = 5.

## Median

In order to calculate the median of the set of data used above, the data must be arranged in order from smallest to largest and then the middle term is the median. The ordered data would appear as 2, 3, 3, 5, 8, 9. Since there are six elements in this data set there is no one value that is in the middle. In this case, the median is the mean of the two middle numbers 3 and 5. So the median is 4. The median has the same number of scores above it as are below it. It can be very useful since it is generally the easiest to understand and is not affected by extremes, which the mean is.

## Mode

A mode is the value that occurs most frequently in a data set. In the data set above the mode is equal to three because it is the only value that occurs twice. It is possible for a set of data to have no mode. It is also possible for a set of data to have more than one mode. Of all three measures of central tendency the mode is considered the least useful. Not only is it possible that it does not reflect the center of the data, but it may not give much information about the data set at all.

### READINGS FOR STUDENTS

Arnold, C. (1984). *Charts and Graphs: Fun, Facts, and Activities.* New York: Franklin Watts.

Brian, S. J. (1999). *Funtastic Math! Probability (Grades 4–8).* New York: Scholastic.

Cushman, J. (1991). *Do You Wanna Bet? Your Chance to Find Out About Probability.* New York: Clarion Books.

Linn, C. (1972). *Probability.* New York: Thomas Y. Crowell Publishers.

Moscovich, I. and Brion, D. (2000). *Mind Games: Probability Games.* New York: Workman.

Murphy, S. J. and Winborn, M. (2001). *Probably Pistachio (Mathstart: Probability, Level 2).* New York: HarperTrophy.

Parker, T. (1984). *In One Day.* Boston: Houghton Mifflin.

## WEBSITES

**Statistics**
www.aaamath.com/B/sta.htm

**Grades 3–5: Data Analysis and Probability**
standards.nctm.org/document/chapter5/data.htm

**SCORE Mathematics Lessons**
score.kings.k12.ca.us/stat.data.prob.html

**ENC: Web Links: Math Topics: Data Analysis and Probability**
Data+Analysis+and+Probability,00.shtm

**Data Analysis and Probability**
www.teachmathmissouri.org/courses/data.htm

**data analysis and probability**
www.teachmathmissouri.org/courses/algebraic.htm

**NCTM Illuminations**
illuminations.nctm.org/standards/

**MA.E.1.4: Mathematics: Data Analysis and Probability**
intech2000.miamisci.org/sss/ma/e14.php3

**Kindergarten Statistics, Data Analysis, and Probability**
www.placercoe.k12.ca.us/archived/pcoe/departments/curriculum/
standards/kind_math.PDF

**National Library of Virtual Manipulatives**
matti.usu.edu/nlvm/nav/topic_t_5.html

**Seeing Math**
seeingmath.concord.org/screenroom.html

**Data Analysis & Probability**
www.madison.k12.wi.us/tnl/math/Probability.PDF

**LHS Programs for Schools: Correlation to the State Standards**
www.lhs.berkeley.edu/pfs/workshopstandards.html

**TUSD Instructional Focus Lessons**
instech.tusd.k12.az.us/focus/twelve/gr12math2.htm

**Data Analysis and Probability**
lessonplancentral.com/lessons/Math/Grades_3_5/Data_Analysis_and_
Probability_/

**Math Forum/USI—Exploring Data**
mathforum.org/workshops/usi/dataproject/usi.elemstds.html

**Let's Make a Deal Math: Probability**
www.cyberbee.com/probability/mathprob.html

**Math Lesson Plans**
mathstar.nmsu.edu/teacher/math_lesson_index.html

**Mission Mastermind: Teacher Pages—National Standards**
amazing-space.stsci.edu/mastermind/teacher/nationalstandards.html

**What Your Child Should be Learning In School—Index**
www.kidsource.com/kidsource/content3/ca.standards/

**Applications in Math**
www.mste.uiuc.edu/presentations/richland99/page2.htm

■ ■ ■ ■ ■

# CHAPTER 10

# PROBLEM SOLVING AND LOGICAL REASONING

Problem solving is the process of following a series of steps to obtain the solution to a problem. The process may be applied to mathematical situations as well as generalized to many different problem situations. When problem solving is mentioned to many children and adults, they usually think of word problems. Problem solving situations often arise from language word problems, but a written problem is not a prerequisite to solving a problem.

## THE PROBLEM SOLVING PROCESS

Many mathematicians have studied how problems are solved. In 1973 George Polya proposed a four-stage model for the problem solving process. The process consists of the following steps:

1. Understand
2. Plan
3. Solve
4. Look Back

Although the steps are numbered, the process is not necessarily linear. As people progress through the steps, they may work on a plan, decide that they need more understanding of the problem, and then go back to step one. Given that ability to move back and forth, most of the work with problem solving uses some variation of these four steps.

Understanding the problem means comprehending the information that has been given, as well as realizing what the problem is asking for. Understanding the problem also means recognizing the information that is missing.

In the planning phase, a strategy is selected that will be followed in order to achieve a solution to the problem. In this second step, prior experience is used to decide what the problem is asking and to select an appropriate plan to attack the problem. The plan will correspond with the person's mathematics knowledge, comfort level, and prior experience with the strategy.

The third step in the process is to use the plan to solve the problem. It is often in this phase that people decide the steps they are taking are not sufficient, and they may retrace to better understand the problem or to develop a different plan. This third step is also where errors in arithmetic may cause an error in the solution, in spite of an appropriate plan.

The last step—looking back—is given the least focus, but it carries extreme importance. In looking back, the person not only "checks" the solution for appropriateness and accuracy, but also examines it for connections to other types of mathematics that have been learned. It is during this step that conceptual understanding continues to develop and that further connections can be made.

## Heuristics

Heuristics is another name for problem solving strategies. These strategies may be applied to a variety of problem situations in order to obtain solutions. The list presented here is not exhaustive, as there are many variations for each strategy listed here:

- Act it Out—Use physical action to model a problem situation.
- Make a Drawing or Diagram—Draw a picture to help depict the information in a problem.
- Look for a Pattern—Identify a pattern and appropriate recursive relationships to determine what comes next.
- Construct a Table—Put the given information into a table to assist in searching for patterns.
- Account for all Possibilities—Look for a pattern and approach this process in a systematic way. This strategy encompasses the previous two strategies.
- Guess and Check—Use prior understanding to make an educated guess about the answer, based on what is known and on prior experiences.
- Work Backward—Use the final condition (when given) as a starting point and proceed backward, step-by-step, until a solution is obtained.

- Write an Open Sentence—Write a sentence or equation to solve the problem. Usually, this is a formal step that leads to algebra.
- Solve a Simpler or Similar Problem—If the whole problem has large numbers or complicated situations, attempt to solve or understand a part of the problem or a simpler problem and then apply that strategy to solving the whole problem. It is also important to consider if the problem is similar to another that has been seen or solved previously. Given this situation, the strategy for the similar problem may be applied.
- Change the Point of View—If a chosen strategy is not bringing satisfactory results, an option is to change to a different strategy. This can be difficult because once people set their mind on following a particular path to reach a solution, it is not always easy or comfortable to change paths.

## Logical Reasoning

Logical reasoning includes the understandings that occur when students begin to classify objects based on identified characteristics. Actually, the act of classifying involves limited logical connections; it is the use of the connectors "and," "or," and "not" that permit these understandings to develop. For example, shapes that are red AND have four sides are classified differently than shapes that are red OR shapes that have four sides. It is through identifying and using these logical connectors that a person builds logical reasoning as well as mathematical understanding.

**READINGS FOR STUDENTS**

Abramson, M. F., Spurgin, R., and Hamilton, L. (2001). *Painless Math Word Problems*. Hauppage, NY: Barrons Education Series.

Allington, R. L., Krull, K., and Garcia, T. (1980). *Thinking*. Milwaukee, WI: Raintree Publications.

Anno, M. (1989). *Anno's Math Games II*. New York: Philomel Books.

Anno, M. and Nozaki, A. (1985). *Anno's Hat Tricks*. New York: Philomel Books.

Axelrod, A. and McGinley-Nally, S. (2000). *Pigs at Odds: Fun with Math & Games*. New York: Simon and Schuster.

Belton, J. and Cramblit, J. (1976). *Domino Games*. Milwaukee, WI: Raintree Publications.

Birch, D. (1998). *The King's Chessboard*. New York: Puffin.

Booth, E. and Collard, D. (1977). *In the Garden*. Milwaukee, WI: Raintree Publications.

Burns, M. (1982). *Math for Smarty Pants*. Boston: Little, Brown.

Butrick, L. M. (1984). *Logic for Space Age Kids*. Athens, OH: University Classics.

Dinio-Durkin, C. (1999). *Brain-boosting Math Activities: Grade 1: More Than 50 Great Activities that Reinforce Problem Solving and Essential Math Skills.* New York: Scholastic.

Draze, D. (1986). *Primarily Problem Solving—Creative Problem Solving Activities.* San Luis Obispo, CA: Dandy Lion Publications.

Frederique, P. and Holding, S. (1971). *Graph Games.* New York: Thomas Y. Crowell Publishers.

Greenes, C., Dacy, L. S., and Spungin, R. (1999). *Estimation and Logical Reasoning (Hot Math Topics: Problem Solving, Communication, and Reasoning Grade 4).* Palo Alto, CA: Dale Seymour Publisher.

Greenes, C., Dacy, L. S., and Spungin, R. (1999). *Geometry and Measurements: Problem Solving, Communication and Reasoning.* Palo Alto, CA: Dale Seymour Publisher.

Greenes, C., Dacy, L. S., and Spungin, R. (1999). *Patterns and Reasoning (Hot Math Topics: Problem Solving, Communication, and Reasoning Grade 3).* Palo Alto, CA: Dale Seymour Publisher.

Greenes, C., Dacy, L. S., and Spungin, R. (1999). *Time and Money (Hot Math Topics: Problem Solving, Communication, and Reasoning).* Palo Alto, CA: Dale Seymour Publisher.

Hayes, C., Hayes D. (1987). *Number Mysteries.* Milwaukee, WI: Penworthy.

Hoban, T. (1978). *Is it Red? Is it Yellow? Is it Blue?* New York: Greenwillow Books.

Lankford, M. D. (1998). *Dominoes around the World.* New York: Morrow Junior Books.

McCall, J. V. and Vydra, J. (1989). *No Problem: Taking the Problem Out of Mathematical Problem Solving.* San Luis Obispo, CA: Dandy Lion Publications.

Ledwon, P. and Mets, M. (2000). *Midnight Math.* New York: Holiday House.

Maisner, H. (1996). *Planet Monster.* Cambridge, MA: Candlewick Press.

Nichols, J. (1999). *Brain-boosting Math Activities—More Than 50 Great Activities That Reinforce Problem-solving and Essential Math Skills: Grade 6.* New York: Scholastic.

Phillips, L. and Stevenson, J. (1985). *263 Brain Busters: Just How Smart are You, Anyway?* New York: Penguin Books.

Tang, G. and Briggs, H. (2001). *The Grapes of Math: Mind Stretching Math Riddles.* New York: Scholastic.

Zaslavsky, C. and Kramer, A. (1982). *Tic Tac Toe.* New York: Thomas Y. Crowell Publishers.

## WEBSITES

**Logical Reasoning**
www.andrews.edu/~calkins/math/webtexts/numb05.htm

**Linda's Activities**
teams.lacoe.edu/documentation/classrooms/linda/geometry/activities/cover.html

**PBS Kids: Cyberchase: For Parents & Teachers: Lessons**
pbskids.org/cyberchase/classroom/lesson6.html

**Logical Reasoning**
www.pinkmonkey.com/studyguides/subjects/gre/part4/gds3p1.htm

**Math Maven's Mysteries**
teacher.scholastic.com/maven/

**Grade Levels and Groupings**
www.greenacres.org/gradelevels.html

**Franklin Elementary Activities**
www.vcsc.k12.in.us/franklin/school%20activities.htm

**Math Games**
www.theteacherscorner.net/math/games/index.htm

**Story Problems**
www.theteacherscorner.net/math/storyproblems/index.htm

**Story Problems**
www.figurethis.org/index40.htm

**Brain Teasers**
www.eduplace.com/math/brain/index.html

**Mathematics Problem Solving—Free Worksheets**
www.rhlschool.com/math.htm

**Grades 6–8: Problem Solving**
standards.nctm.org/document/chapter6/prob.htm

**EMAT 4600/6600 Page**
jwilson.coe.uga.edu/emt725/EMT725.html

**Mathematics Problem Solving Task Centres**
www.mav.vic.edu.au/PSTC/

**Problem Solving Strategies**
mathcounts.org/Problems/strategies.html

**MATHCOUNTS Home Page**
mathcounts.org/

**Mathematical Problems—Problem Solving**
www.abc.se/~m9847/matre/problem.html

**Problem Solving in Mathematics**
jersey.uoregon.edu/~chuckp/

**Problem Solving**
web.mit.edu/efedula/Public/solve.html

**Math Forum: MathMagic!**
mathforum.org/mathmagic/

**Word Problems For Kids**
www.stfx.ca/special/mathproblems/

**Math Word Problems for Children**
www.mathstories.com/

**Math Goodies: Free Interactive Math Lessons, Homework Help**
www.mathgoodies.com/

**Mathematics and Science Education Center—Math Problem Solving**
www.nwrel.org/msec/mpm/

**Brain Teasers**
www.eduplace.com/math/brain/

**Math Problem Solving, Volumes 1–3**
www.rhlschool.com/mathv1–3.htm

**Teacher Talk 3(2): Great Ideas—"Problem Solving Skills Builder"**
education.indiana.edu/cas/tt/v3i2/probsolve.html

**Math Problem Solving**
www.abcteach.com/ProblemSolving/PSMenu.htm

**Mathematics Through Problem Solving**
www.mathgoodies.com/articles/problem_solving.shtm

**Teaching Tips for TAs: Teaching Problem Solving**
www.id.ucsb.edu/IC/TA/tips/prob.html

**Problem Solving Activities**
www.madison.k12.wi.us/toki/probsolv.htm

**Problem Solving**
www.nzmaths.co.nz/PS/

**TIP: Theories**
tip.psychology.org/schoen.html

**Practicing Problem Solving (Lesson Plan)**
teachervision.com/lesson-plans/lesson-3025.html

▪ ▪ ▪ ▪ ▪

# CHAPTER 11

# MATHEMATICS, TECHNOLOGY, AND TEACHING

Technology is the use of knowledge to create tools people can use—including past developments and today's most sophisticated inventions. Earliest humans invented simple technology long before humankind had grasped some of the most important mathematical concepts. With humankind's increased understanding of mathematics, there have been concomitantly sophisticated inventions.

Although the natural world existed long before both people and technology, the observations and data recorded from the time of the ancients through increasingly careful processes and habits of mind has meant that the history of humankind has been in large part a history of ever more complex technology. Although the natural world is too big and too complex for the human mind to completely encompass, once people recognized that many natural events occur in consistent, recognizable patterns, which often appeared in mathematical constructs, they could put that knowledge to use in solving problems and creating technology.

The teaching of mathematics has changed dramatically in one particular area in the past ten years—the use of technology. While content knowledge is paramount for teachers, delivery of that knowledge is very different than in the past. It is incumbent upon the teacher to learn to use the available technology, since mathematics and technology are perfect partners in educating students.

Technology can be as "low tech" as the very popular manipulatives that students use to learn important math concepts, but more commonly, it refers to television, videos, videodiscs, DVDs, calculators, computers, computer based instructional tools, computer software, CD-ROMS, and the Internet. However, as with any tool, the teacher needs to choose the appropriate technology with the purpose of enhancing the learning of mathematics, not just for the sake of using technology.

Teachers need to be able to successfully operate the technology of choice and be familiar with a wide range of resources to use with the chosen tool. They should be able to critically evaluate the strengths and weaknesses of the technologies and resources they use, and to assess how well those two things relate to the mathematics lessons being taught, keeping in mind subject matter, student diversity, and instructional strategies. Factors to be evaluated should include the knowledge and experience of the creators of the technological tool being used, the purpose and goals of the resource, the suitability for students, the utility of the math topic under study, connections to additional resources, and reviews by other educators.

Computers will probably be the most common technology in the elementary classroom. Teachers should be able to demonstrate the use of computers for problem-solving, analyzing data bases (including data collections and management), communicating, presenting, and graphing utilities—while simultaneously applying current knowledge about instruction and assessments to the use of various instructional technologies. Teachers also need to keep up to date on the educational uses of technologies, to enhance personal and professional productivity of themselves, in addition to facilitating for their students.

## READINGS FOR STUDENTS

Adler, D. A. and Oberman, A. and Oberman, M. (1981). *Calculator fun.* New York: Franklin Watts.

Flansburg, S. (1998). *Math Magic for Your Kids: Hundreds of Games and Exercises from the Human Calculator to Make Math Fun and Easy.* New York: HarperCollins.

Haney, C. (1983). *Calculators.* Milwaukee, WI: Raintree Publications.

Lear, P. and Migliore, R. (1985). *Let's Look at Computer Play.* Burlington, Ontario: Hayes Publishing.

Lipscomb, S. D. and Zuanich, M. A. (1982). *BASIC Fun: Computer Games, Puzzles, and Problems Children can Write.* New York: Avon.

Lipson, S. and Stapleton, J. (1982). *It's Basic: The ABC's of Computer Programming.* New York: Holt, Rinehart & Winston.

Mackie, D., Mackie D., and Migliore, R. (1985). *Let's look at Basic.* Burlington, Ontario: Hayes Publishing.

**WEBSITES**

**Technology Integration**
www.learning.com/

**Web as Medium for Learning Math**
www.beritsbest.com/SeriousStuff/Math/index.shtml

**Directory of Web Math Resources**
www.pitt.edu/~poole/

**Internet-based Education Materials**
search.thegateway.org/

**Using Educational Technology**
4teachers.org

**Video Math Resources**
www.evrmath.com/

**Interactive Lessons, Homework, Worksheets**
www.mathgoodies.com/

**Elementary Math Methods—Math Links**
www.educ.drake.edu/espey/math/math-links.htm

**PBS TeacherSource—Teaching & Technology**
www.pbs.org/teachersource/teachtech.htm

**Science, Math and Educational Technology Resources**
jan.ucc.nau.edu/~lrm22/

**Science Math Technology**
hometown.aol.com/scimate2/

**Center for Science, Mathematics, and Technology Education**
www.eastnet.ecu.edu/outreach/CSMTE/

**Math, Science, and Technology Programs for Girls**
www.aauw.org/2000/modelsbd.html

**The School Page—The MATH Page**
www.eyesoftime.com/teacher/math.htm

**Children's Science, Math, and Tech Books at Embracing the Child**
www.embracingthechild.com/Booksciencetech.htm

**Integrating Math and Technology**
www.manassas.k12.va.us/tech/training/resources/Math/integrating_math
_and_technology.htm

**Mathematics Resources**
www.educationindex.com/math/

**Science & Math—FirstGov for Kids**
www.kids.gov/k_science.htm

**The Technology Education Lab: K–12 Educational Resources**
www.techedlab.com/k12.html

**Girls, Science, and Math Education Links**
www.ehr.nsf.gov/ehr/hrd/ge/girls-rev.html

**The Math Forum—Math Library—Articles**
mathforum.org/library/resource_types/articles/

**IUP Teacher Education Center for Science and Mathematics**
www.iup.edu/smetc/

# CHAPTER 12

# COMMUNICATION, CONNECTIONS, AND REPRESENTATION

The Principles and Standards for School Mathematics (2001) express the importance that communication, connections, and representations play in the understanding of mathematics.

## COMMUNICATION

The various ways that people convey information make up communication. Children spend a lot of time learning how to read, write, and speak to one another in order to communicate clearly. This same focus needs to be placed on communicating mathematically.

### Vocabulary

Understanding of the definitions of mathematical terms is essential to developing competence with mathematics. Mathematics requires a precise language. There has been some discussion in recent years about whether the vocabulary needs precision, or whether it should develop using more familiar children's words and understandings. To this end, many adults have been short changed because there was not a requirement for the development and refinement of their mathematical vocabulary; rather, it was left in the early stages. While the early stage is a fine place for vocabulary to begin, one must continue to learn and refine one's understanding and proper use of the vocabulary.

Just like any language, mathematics has unique terms. Addition, square root, polynomial, quadrilateral, and countless other terms have precise definitions and contexts in which their uses are correct. One must learn these in order to communicate mathematics correctly and effectively.

## Talking

Given appropriate understanding and use of mathematical vocabulary, learning to verbally communicate about mathematics is another area of communication that needs to be developed. In talking about mathematics to another person, one must convey his or her understanding of the context and the situation. Teachers must know how to talk about mathematics and to explain not only what they are doing, but why. For teachers, listening to another's response is even more important than stating the words. It is the ability to interpret this response and then reply in turn in an appropriate fashion that gives the teacher or student the ability to communicate mathematics verbally. Therefore, listening and discerning the congruence of a reply are as important in the communication process as being able to effectively construct a statement.

## Writing

Not only does mathematics have vocabulary that is specific to the discipline, but it has many symbols and notational rules as well. For example, one must know what a "+" mark means, as well as know the rules that govern its use. For example, a person may correctly write 3 + 14 + 6, but he or she may not correctly write 3 = 14 = 6. It is through practice that the understanding of these symbols becomes second nature, rather than the focal point of the mathematics. When this understanding becomes second nature, the student is able to move to focusing on understanding the mathematical concepts.

## Reading

As with writing, in "reading mathematics" an understanding of the symbols and of how they are used is essential. There are two types of mathematical reading that occur. The first is the reading of the numerals, symbols, and algorithms. The second is reading the words that describe mathematical situations and procedures. The ability to read these two types of mathematical communication is essential to a person's mathematical development.

## CONNECTIONS

Showing students the connections between mathematics and other subjects, as well as within the subject of mathematics, is important so that mathematics is not studied in isolation. The concepts that are learned can be connected with other familiar ideas. This intellectual connection is as important in mathematics as it is in other subjects.

### Connections with Other Subjects

There are many obvious connections between mathematics and other subjects, and there are some that may not be so obvious. For example, measurement is learned mathematics. This is also a skill used in science, cooking, sewing, and geography. Computation is used in scientific experimentation and many areas of the social sciences. Geometry is an obvious part of art and architecture. Musical compositions consist of notes that have various fractional values. Throughout the daily paper, tables, charts, and graphs give information and describe situations that could not be interpreted without a knowledge of mathematics. All of these areas and more can be easily identified.

An area that may not be as obvious is the rhyming pattern present in some literature, such as the iambic pentameter in English poetry, based on a specific number of syllables per line. Through understanding patterns and relationships in reading or speaking, a person learns to anticipate the value that will come next. The application of mathematical thought to many daily situations helps the person base next steps on what has previously occurred. Mathematics has countless connections.

### Connections within Mathematics

There are also connections that exist within mathematics, many of which have been mentioned in this book. Multiplication can be thought of as repeated addition and division can be thought of as repeated subtraction. Fractions are related to whole numbers and also are related to decimals, and decimals are related to whole numbers and to fractions...and to percents. It is these connections that are made throughout the study of mathematics that enable the development of mathematical understanding.

## REPRESENTATION

A representation is an image or a likeness of something. Mathematical concepts that are connected to models are examples of representations. For example, five cubes are a representation of the number five. Concrete objects often aid the development of mathematical understanding because they provide a physical object to which the mathematical concept and language can connect. In many cases, the more representations that are associated with a concept, the better or more completely that concept is developed and understood. One example of the strength of representation occurs in algebra. Through the use of tables, graphs, and equations, an algebraic situation can be described in multiple formats with meaning developed in each.

## COMMUNICATION, CONNECTIONS, AND REPRESENTATION

The areas of communication, connections, and representation are not topical areas in mathematics, but habits of mathematics and clear, logical mathematical thinking that are essential to the development of mathematical understanding.

### READINGS FOR STUDENTS

Berry, D. (1994). *The Rajah's Rice: A Mathematical Folktale from India*. New York: W. H. Freeman and Company.

Diagram Group. (1980). *Comparisons*. New York: St. Martin's Press.

Paulos, J. A. (1989). *Innumeracy*. New York: Hill and Wang.

Reimer, L. and Reimer, W. (1990). *Mathematicians are People, Too*, 2 vols. Palo Alto, CA: Dale Seymour Publications.

Scieszka, J. and Smith, L. (1995). *Math Curse*. New York: Penguin.

### WEBSITES

**Literacy Coalition—Literacy and Internet Resources**
dmla.clan.lib.nv.us/docs/nsla/literacy/it-resources.htm

**Dynamyte Use in the Classroom—Quicktime Version**
www.bownet.org/pt3/video/NewBoston/DynamyteQT.htm

**Student Progress**
www.bham.wednet.edu/schlinfo/Student%20Progress.html

**Core 3 Part 2 Activity 3 Searching Sites**
www.learningspace.org/prof_growth/training/research/s3sites.html

**SU [Seidel School—TRC—Online Educational Resources]**
trc.salisbury.edu/Resources/math.html

**Math Lesson Plans**
www.kent.k12.wa.us/curriculum/math/teachers.html

**KidCode: A Community Tool to Support Collaborative Learning**
www.ciltkn.org/cilt2000/abstracts/2042.html

# A FINAL WORD

This book is intended to help give teachers the impetus and the confidence to encourage their students' interest in mathematics, and to teach competently and engagingly the lessons that are so often perfunctory in mathematics at the elementary level. Whether the reason for the widespread dislike of mathematics is lack of knowledge or interest on the teacher's part, or simply the pervasive time constraints of language arts and "specials," mathematics should be an inspiring part of the curriculum. Every child should have the opportunity to develop interest in and knowledge of mathematical concepts and applications, not least because calculus is the gateway to many college majors.

Clearly, there are omissions in this book—some deliberate because of space constraints, some inadvertent. The resource guide may help those who would like to pursue overlooked areas of study or further understand the topics discussed. Some of the information may be outdated before this book is published, but one of the joys of study is the wonderful torrent of new and continuous information. With the attention on the study of the humanities that began with the Greeks, was reborn in the Renaissance, and spiraled in the "Age of Enlightenment"—mathematics established itself as a vitally important field of study. Through the years, the accumulation of mathematical knowledge and application has contributed to many of humankind's endeavors, echoing Francis Bacon's dictum that true knowledge is useful knowledge.

Much of life is concerned with mathematics, as it relates to so many applications, from measuring for paint or carpeting to helping create advanced technology. This book aspires to lay the foundation for the teacher to help open that remarkable accumulation of knowledge, to pique the interest and encourage the knowledge of the teacher, and through the teacher, to give the student the great gift of being a thinking and numerate participant in the world.

# GENERAL RESOURCES
# FOR THE TEACHER

Note: Content-specific resources for students can be found at the end of each chapter, along with content-specific websites appropriate for both students and teachers.

There are many thousands of books, articles, and various other resources, including software and websites. From the plethora of materials available, there are some idiosyncratic favorites the teacher may deem helpful. Undoubtedly, the teacher will find many good selections beyond this list, particularly in the mushrooming websites and the constant flow of new children's books. There are also many good mathematics books easily found in libraries and media centers by particular subject area name. In addition to the following general resources, specific suggestions are given at the end of each chapter.

The National Council of Teachers of Mathematics (NCTM) (1906 Association Drive, Reston, VA 20191-1502 and on the web at nctm.org) was founded in 1920 and has over 100,000 members. The organization publishes the teacher-oriented journals *Teaching Children Mathematics, Mathematics Teaching in the Middle School, Mathematics Teacher,* and *Journal for Research in Mathematics Education,* which contain helpful articles each month on teaching various math content. In addition to selling the national standards and posting them on the website, NCTM also publishes and sells many valuable individual books and support materials that the teacher may find helpful. The catalogue is available at www.nctm.org/catalog.

The elementary or middle school teacher who cares about content will find a classroom encyclopedia, either hardcopy or electronic, indispensable for answering the inevitable student questions on far-flung mathematics material, and may also wish to acquire high school level textbooks as resources in the various content areas from the district school book depository. Dover Books (31 East 2nd Street, Mineola, NY 11501) and Bellerophon Books (36 Anacapa Street, Santa Barbara, CA 93101) are particularly fine resources for math-related special interest books, coloring books, concept building kits, and other similar materials. Minnesota Educational Computing Corporation (MECC at 6160 Summit Drive North, Minneapolis, MN 55430) and Tom Snyder Productions (80 Collidge Hill Road, Watertown, MA 02172) are among the leaders in producing school software in all content areas, including math.

## Comprehensive, descriptive, and analytic sources for children's literature relevant to mathematics concepts include those below:

Bresser, R. (1995). *Math and Literature, Grades 4–6.* Sausalito, CA: Math Solutions Publications.

Burns, M. (1993). *Math and Literature, Grades K–3, Book One.* Sausalito, CA: Math Solutions Publications.

Norton, D. (2001. *Through the Eyes of a Child: An Introduction to Children's Literature.* 6th ed. Upper Saddle River, NJ: Merrill Prentice-Hall.

Sheffield, S. (1995). *Math and Literature, Grades K–3, Book One.* Sausalito, CA: Math Solutions Publications.

Tomlinson, C. M. and Lynch-Brown, C. (1996). *Essentials of Children's Literature.* 2nd edition. Boston, MA: Allyn & Bacon.

Welchman-Tischler, R. (1992). *How to Use Children's Literature to Teach Mathematics.* Reston, VA: The National Council of Teachers of Mathematics.

## Good, general overviews of school mathematics include those below:

Abramson, M. F., Spungin, R., and Hamilton, L. (2001). *Painless Math Word Problems.* Hauppage, NY: Barrons Educational Series.

Baratta-Lorton, M. (1994). *Math Their Way: Complete Revised Anniversary Edition.* Glenview, IL: Pearson Learning.

Hager, E., Meyers, R., and Torrance, E. P. (1996). *Cognitive Connections: Multiple Ways of Thinking With Math.* Tucson, AZ: Zephyr Press.

Helton, S. M. and Micklo, S. (1997). *The Elementary Math Teacher's Book of Lists: With Ready-To-Use Patterns and Worksheets.* Hoboken, NJ: Jossey-Bass.

Howett, J. (2000). *Contempory's Number Power 1: A Real World Approach to Math: Addition, Subtraction, Multiplication, and Division.* New York: McGraw Hill/Contemporary Books.

Jacobs, J. E. and Rossi Becker, J. (Eds.) (2000). *Changing the Faces of Mathematics: Perspectives on Gender Equity.* Reston, VA: National Council of Teachers of Mathematics.

Lewis, S. (2001). *Teacher, I'm done! Now What Do I Do: Over 80 Math Puzzles, Word Plays, and Brainteasers.* Huntingdon Beach, CA: Creative Teaching Press.

Micklo, S. J. and Beresin, A. (2001). *Primary Teacher's Math Activities Kit: Includes Over 100 Ready-To-Use Lessons and Activity Sheets Covering Six Areas of the K–3 Math Curriculum.* Norwich, U.K.: Center for Applied Research in Education.

Muschla, J. A. (1998). *Math Starters!: 5 to 10 Minute Activities That Make Kids Think, Grades 6–12.* Hoboken, NJ: Jossey-Bass.

Thiessen, D., Matthias, M., & Smith, J. (1998). *The Wonderful World of Mathematics.* Reston, VA: The National Council of Teachers of Mathematics.

Zeman, A. and Kelly, K. (1994). *Everything You Need to Know about Math Homework.* New York: Scholastic.

## WEBSITES FOR TEACHERS

**National Council of Teachers of Mathematics**
www.nctm.org

**Math information K–12**
forum.swarthmore.edu

**Math and Science Standard, Data, Resources, Websites**
www.enc.org

**Curriculum, Resources, and Lesson Plans**
teachers.net

**Lesson Plans**
www.theteacherscorner.net/math/index.htm

**Mini-lessons/Elementary**
ofcn.org/cyber.serv/academy/ace/math/elem.html

**Mini-lessons/Intermediate**
ofcn.org/cyber.serv/academy/ace/math/inter.html

**Lesson Plans**
www.lessonplanspage.com/Math.htm

**Math is Everywhere**
gpn.unl.edu/rainbow/booklist/booklist.asp

**Lesson Plans**
enc.org/weblinks/math/

**Math Skills/Practical Applications**
www.bottco.com/Schoolsite/MATH.html

**Review of Sites**
archives.math.utk.edu/k12.html

**Data Base of Lesson Plans/Resources**
www.educationplanet.com/search/Math

**Math Education Resources**
mathforum.org/

**Math Directory**
www.yahooligans.com/School_Bell/Math/

**Math Links for Teachers**
www.sitesforteachers.com/resources_sharp/math/math.html

**Resources**
www.theteacherscorner.net/math/miscellaneous/index.htm

# INDEX